Extreme Esteem The Four Factors

Murray Fuhrer

Murray M. Fuhrer

Extreme Esteem Publishing
Red Deer Alberta Canada

Edited by Carl R. Hahn with foreword by Glenn H. Allen

Cover design by Brenda A. Kolasa – Visual Resolve Graphics, Red Deer, Alberta
www.visualresolvegraphics.com

Back cover photograph by John H. Read Photography, Red Deer, Alberta
www.johnhreadphotography.com

Printed and bound in Canada by Blitzprint, Calgary, Alberta
www.blitzprint.com
Library and Archives Canada Cataloguing in Publication
Fuhrer, Murray M., 1957-
Extreme Esteem: The Four Factors: four components of empowered living / Murray M. Fuhrer.
Originally published in a weekly newspaper column.
ISBN 13: 978-0-9739017-0-2
1. Self-esteem. 2. Self-actualization (Psychology). I. Title.
BF697.5.S46F83 2007 158.1 C2007-905642-3

Published in Canada by Extreme Esteem Publishing – Red Deer, Alberta.

For more information on this volume or other Extreme Esteem publications or to arrange for an author interview or use a quote, visit the website at www.extremeesteem.ca

Dedication

For my wife, Elke: my inspiration, grounding force, and my confidante. For my children – the expression of family, meaning, and purpose. For my granddaughter, Alexis – the personification of possibilities and hope. And for my mother, Eileen Fuhrer, whose gentle guidance and encouragement laid the foundation for a fulfilling and meaningful life.

"I write entirely to find out what I'm thinking, what I'm looking at, what I see, and what it means. What I want and what I fear."

– Joan Didion, author and journalist

Contents

Acknowledgements

I am deeply grateful to the many people who contributed time, energy, and ideas to this book. First, all my love to my immediate family, my wife, Elke, and my wonderful mother, Eileen Fuhrer. I would never be in the enviable position I am now without the love and support of each of you. It is for you that I strive to reach for the stars.

There would never have been a book or a first column for that matter without my editor and good friend, Carl Hahn. Carl is the former editor of the *Red Deer Advocate Life* publications and was the first to show interest in my self-esteem column. I give thanks to Carl for his faith in me and for constantly demanding that I write cleaner and tighter, and more fully consider each thought and every concept before committing it to a final draft.

The advice and encouragement of mentors Glenn Allen, Wendy and Kelly Collier along with members of the Self-Esteem Society for Central Alberta have been invaluable and a constant source of inspiration. Writers need the support of fellow writers, and each week my friends and colleagues at Writers' Ink – The Red Deer & District Writers' Club listen to me read my columns, then provide me with insights and cheer my successes.

Whether I'm hosting a workshop, a stage presentation, giving a talk, or launching a new project, I can always count on the help of Rhonda Morison, Pamela Klatt, Sheila Horn, and Crystal Gall. These angels have gone out of their way to help me spread the message of self-esteem and empowerment throughout Central Alberta and beyond.

Hats off to my fellow writer and Sunday coffee buddy David White and to my oldest and dearest friend Lorne Starko. You've never been afraid to offer advice, ask the tough questions, or challenge me to push myself to the next level. Thanks guys!

I wanted a great picture for the back cover so sought the talent of Big John of John Read Photography. For a cover that was truly impressive, I commissioned graphic artists Carla Howard, who created the initial concept, and Brenda Kolasa, who finalized the design. Wow. You all exceeded my expectations. Thank you!

Over the years, many people expressed to me a desire for one-on-one counseling. Dr. James Baker encouraged me to set up an empowerment practice at his clinic, The Baker Wellness Center in Red Deer, Alberta. The experience has been profoundly life-changing and I thank you deeply James for your kindness. Mike Fletcher and Dawn Smith of Neworld Coaching in Stratford, Ontario are tremendously successful life and business coaches. Thank you for the offer to market my book and for your many "Get that damn book done!" emails.

Of course, a special expression of gratitude goes to all the participants of my many workshops who invariably teach me more than I ever teach them. As well, warmest regards to all the people who invite me out to speak or facilitate, to those who email me, call me, write me letters, attach a column to the fridge or even approach me on the street, like a woman did recently outside a local restaurant.

"You're Murray, right?" she asked, and I nodded. "I read your column every week," she declared. "You have no idea the difference you're making in the world."

Again, with the deepest thanks and so much love, I thank each of you once more.

Murray M. Fuhrer

Foreword

For many people self-esteem fluctuates over time. Some have a general sense of efficacy that can sustain them through periods of decline. Many, however, need consistent reminders of how to make a difference in their perception of self. Often I have thought a daily or even weekly reminder of what was important would help me "hold the point" and sustain my self-esteem. When Murray Fuhrer began to visit my psyche, in the form of a weekly column in our local newspaper, my need was met. I began a ritual of revitalizing myself through Murray's wisdom. It was like a fitness regime for my body, except the weekly workout was for my mind.

In *The Four Factors*, Murray has assembled more than 100 of his best columns. Now, with so many in one volume, I can read one, several or all, as I need or desire. The content is exciting, informative and energizing. He writes with a candor that is educational, and just as easily entertaining. Most columns contain not only practical information but poignant illustrations taken from the author's own life journey. Such a linkage is unique. The learning is enhanced because it is so easy to relate to his stories and metaphors. It is as if his own tales belong in our scenario.

Several years ago Murray was invited to speak to a community organization focused on developing healthy self-esteem. Although his expertise lay in hypnosis and wellness, his knowledge and understanding of self-esteem was apparent from the beginning. Participants were thrilled with his teaching. So began a long-standing relationship between the society and this man. A leader and a teacher who has come into his time, Murray has successfully orchestrated the growth of his company, Extreme Esteem, and has attained another new level with this book. I know you will learn and enjoy. Your sense of value and capability will be enhanced.

Glenn Allen
Founder of The Self Esteem Society for Central Alberta

Preface

Before there was ever an Extreme Esteem column or a workshop, there was my unshakable belief that the powerful message of self-esteem and empowerment needed to be seen, heard, read, and experienced. Looking back, I had no idea writing a column would put me onto a purposeful path and launch me into an entirely new career: that of a professional writer, speaker, and facilitator of self-esteem and empowerment workshops.

I had long entertained the idea of writing a self-esteem, self-awareness column for the local newspaper, but lacked a clear focus – a solid foundation upon which to build the concept. The idea grew out of my own need to find meaning in my life and the desire to live a life of passion and purpose. After a couple of misfires and more than a few rejections, I sat down in 2003 with then *Red Deer Life* editor, and now good friend, Carl Hahn. I told Carl I wanted to write a column that would make a difference in the life of the reader. Perhaps Carl thought the idea was a bit grandiose – I don't know – but he didn't discourage me. In fact, he looked me in the eye and said, "Show me what you've got."

I emailed Carl six columns fashioned under the working title *Thoughts Along the Path*. Carl read them and promptly responded with a firm, "Nope." He told me people want grounded concepts, not "airy-fairy" notions. They want believable, real-life people and situations they can relate to. Carl wanted a column people would clip out and post on the fridge or bulletin board – a column readers would happily share with friends.

A little discouraged, yet still hopeful, I went back to the keyboard. I rewrote a couple of new columns and returned them to Carl. He read over them and responded. "Now we have something," he said. "Write me six columns in total and have them back to me in a couple of weeks." Carl needed to confirm that I had enough workable material to sustain the concept. The last thing he wanted was to launch a column that fizzled out after a few installments. I wrote 10 columns under the new working title *Extreme Esteem* and had them back to Carl within a week.

"Let's do it," he said. "I'll write an introduction and you write your philosophy." Carl wrote these phrases in the introduction, which still describe the column accurately today.

Think of it as your weekly pick-me-up, with no caffeine added.... Each week in LIFE, Murray will provide thoughtful and practical insights and advice to help build your self-esteem and uncover your true potential.

I wrote the following column.

I am convinced that low self-esteem is the common thread in most, and perhaps all, personal distress. Some problems are a direct expression of underdeveloped self-esteem: shyness, timidity, fear of self-assertion, intimacy, or human relationships, and lack of participation in life. Other issues can be understood as defenses against the reality of the problem: controlling and manipulative behavior, obsessive-compulsive disorders, inappropriate aggressiveness, and destructive forms of ambition. All of these consequences are driven by the desire to experience worth, control, and personal value.

A good question to ask might be, "How do I feel about myself when I avoid a challenging issue, and how do I feel when I confront the threatening issue?" In other words, how do my choices and actions affect how I feel about myself?

Self-esteem is the experience of being competent to cope with the basic challenges of life and feeling worthy of happiness. It consists of two components: (1) Confidence in your ability to think, learn, choose, and make appropriate decisions, and, ultimately, to master challenges and manage change; and (2) Self-respect – confidence in your right to be happy and, therefore, deserving of success, friendship, respect, love and fulfillment.

How we feel about ourselves impacts every moment of our lives. Self-evaluation is the basis upon which we act and react, choose our values, set our goals, and meet the challenges of life. Who and what we think we are, how competent and worthy we perceive ourselves as being, shapes our responses to events. Of all the judgments we pass in life, none is more significant than the judgment we pass upon ourselves.

Positive self-esteem operates as our emotional immune system, providing resistance, strength, and a capacity for regeneration. In the same way a strong physical immune system defends us against disease, our emotional immune system helps us to feel secure and confident in times of stress and allows us to respond appropriately to challenges and opportunities. Positive self-esteem empowers, energizes, and motivates us to greatness.

Since that initial column and to the point of bringing out this volume, I have had over 200 columns published with no shortage of topics in sight. The longer I study and write on the subject of self-esteem and empowerment, the more I grow in my own awareness and the greater my desire to share these powerful concepts and ideas with the public.

I'm reminded of the words of Joseph Campbell, American folklorist who once wrote, "When you follow your bliss, doors will open where you would not have thought there would be doors and where there wouldn't be a door for anyone else."

May you follow your bliss as I continue to follow mine.

"Do not believe that he who seeks to comfort you lives untroubled among the simple and quiet words that sometimes do you good. His life has much difficulty. Were it otherwise, he would never have been able to find those words."

– Rainer Maria Rilke, 20th Century German poet

Introduction

I guess I've always been a ponderer. Is that a word? It's certainly a state of being. When I look back at old photographs, I'm laughing, smiling, or sitting there with a perplexed look on my face, my brow furrowed, my eyes narrowed to slits – pondering.

As a child, I was forever taking things apart to see what made them work. It was only natural that my pondering would eventually turn toward people, life, and myself.

I began to ponder why people said the things they said, why they did the things they did, and why words and the behaviors I witnessed were often contradictory. I learned at a young age that truth could often be found in behavior. People could tell me whatever they wanted but, if I watched them carefully, I would soon observe what they truly believed. I remember my father talking to me about the hazards of smoking while deftly rolling a cigarette paper between his thumb, index and middle fingers. I became aware of a "disconnect" between espoused values and outward behavior. As much as we might intellectualize about why change is necessary or beneficial, we don't often do it.

If we can know something intellectually and explain it in detail, why do we often choose to continue travelling the well-rutted road of our past? What keeps us stuck? My first real glimpse into the inner workings of the mind came in high school when I had the opportunity to work backstage with Canada's premier hypnotist, M. Vance Romane. I was intrigued by the subconscious component of the mind and the seeming power it had over conscious behavior. In trance, an experience suggested by the hypnotist could be played out in reality. I began to ponder whether a thought held firmly in mind could produce a predictable outcome in life. I began to realize that beliefs or values formed at an early age often functioned below the level of conscious awareness and influenced our actions.

I have since learned that about 80 percent of our programming – beliefs and values – are in place by the time we're 10 years of age, and few of us ever reexamine them.

Over the years, my ponderings have brought to light some surprising discoveries about why my own life has unfolded in the manner it has. With such knowledge came an understanding of how issues in the lives of other people came into being. I have discovered – despite our different backgrounds – that we have more in common than ever imagined.

That's what this book is really about: my journey through fear, confusion and regret, to a place of love, awareness, and empowerment. I've had some powerful teachers along the way – people whose wisdom and insights were beyond my understanding at the time. I think many of these people were unaware of the lessons they were teaching – either by word or by behavior. Maybe that's the way it is for most of us. Perhaps intuitively, we know there is something of value in a certain experience, so we tuck it away until the point when we can take it out, ponder it further, and bring some understanding to the words and events. You'll meet some amazing people in the pages ahead. As you experience their words and wisdom, I encourage you to flip through the pages of your own past. I'm certain you'll find many teachers there and a bounty of wisdom and insight.

People often ask me, "What is self-esteem?" Here's how I've come to understand it. Take the phrase "self-esteem" and break it into two words. If you esteem someone, you hold him or her in high regard. You like that person. You trust that person. You would have faith in the individual and enjoy his or her companionship. If asked, you would certainly say the esteemed individual is deserving of success and happiness in life.

Now let's add the word "self" back into the equation – "self" simply being you. When you have good self-esteem, you esteem yourself: you have faith in you. You like yourself, trust in your abilities, and hold yourself in high regard. You feel truly deserving of success and happiness. For most people, the "self" component is absent from the equation.

When it comes to putting the "self" back in self-esteem, there is no magic process. All it takes is a genuine desire to change and a series of practical steps to make change occur.

Buddha said, "You can search throughout the entire universe for someone who is more deserving of your love and affection than you are yourself, and that person is not to be found anywhere." That is the essence of self-esteem and the true path to empowerment.

The writing of each column in this book has been an outcropping of my genuine desire to bring about positive and needed change in my life – essentially, to put my "self" back into the equation. Often, I would purposefully choose to write on a theme that I had never fully explored so that I could investigate it, ponder it and, in the end, decide where I stood on the subject. Readers have often said to me, "I wish I had come to the realization years ago that you so wonderfully captured in your last column." I wish I had, too.

I've called the first half of the book *Two Steps Back* as I'm asking you to become the witness and to view your life experiences from a different point of view. Figuratively speaking, I'm challenging you to step outside of your own skin – to move beyond your fears and prejudices and view your life experience from the standpoint of an objective observer. Doing so will help you see how certain beliefs and values were formed and how each has continued to play a pivotal role in your current life experience.

By and large, an individual brought up in a loving and nurturing environment will start out life with a positive self-image. Over time, that individual will build upon positive early programming by focusing on positive and empowering experiences – the success stories. But if the early programming is negative, the individual will build upon that; thus the first two factors can become two steps back, away from establishing and maintaining healthy self-esteem.

I call the first factor *Early Programming*. Though some may assert that we each come into the world with a genetic predisposition – and I would not argue the point, being the father of five children – few can dispute the impact that early programming has had or still has upon our life experience. Whether you were raised in a loving, nurturing environment or a harsh and fearful atmosphere, the words spoken and messages received formed the foundation upon which you have built your life. In Factor Number One, we'll reexamine past experiences, learn ways to embrace the positive and release or reframe the negative so we are no longer bound by programming that hinders our development.

The second factor is *Reinforcement of Belief*. Essentially, once we have chosen to embrace a particular view of life, we begin to filter our experiences to support the belief. The more that a negative or positive aspect is affirmed, the more power it has to create fear or joy in our lives. You will come to understand how the whole world is really just your story projected back to you on the screen of your own perception. In Factor Number Two, we'll learn how beliefs are reinforced – the way in which we "cherry pick" events to support our perceptions, for better or for worse

– and how, with awareness, we can break the cycle of negative reinforcement and choose a grounded, positive outlook.

The second section is called *Two Steps Forward,* as the challenge becomes to accept responsibility for our life and choose a better and more empowered path. We take two steps back to gain perspective – to reclaim our lost steps. We take two steps forward to begin the journey anew – our eyes to the future, our focus on the now, anchored in the moment.

The third factor is *Self-Responsibility*. As you awaken and become aware of all the possibilities life holds for you, you'll need to make a choice: to stay with your current beliefs and level of discomfort, or to walk free. I'm willing to wager you'll walk free. In writing the columns and later this book, I found a tremendous focus on the aspect of self-responsibility. Certainly, without self-responsibility the first action step will never happen. Self-responsibility means owning the gap between your current state and your ideal outcome. In Factor Three, you'll discover ways to initiate and sustain forward momentum by taking accountability for your life. In effect, the buck stops with you.

The final factor is *Effecting Change*. While awareness is always the first step to understanding the self, awareness alone does not bring about positive change in your life. The key to transforming your life is to learn what it means to accept and embrace yourself. Psychologist Carl Rogers drew the same conclusion when he wrote, "The curious paradox is that when I accept myself just as I am, then I can change."

If you begin to understand who you are without trying to change it, then what you are undergoes a transformation. Acceptance provides us with a starting point. It is then that positive change will actually occur, by assuming self-responsibility and persistently applying new thoughts, ideas, and insights.

I have chosen not to offer a long and drawn-out summary at the conclusion of each section as I feel each column is a self-contained lesson in esteem-building. I have, however, posed a number of questions and statements at the close of each section that you may ponder alone or with a group of equally inspired individuals. Honestly responding to each question and statement will provide a starting point on your journey of self-discovery.

Around the world, people are awakening to their spirituality. Although joyous and liberating, it can also be confusing, sometimes frightening, and often painful. Sharing your experiences helps not only yourself but others, too.

I hope sharing these thoughts, ideas, and suggestions will aid you in choosing a path that leads toward an empowered life and the realization of your own unique purpose.

Recently, someone said to me, "Your life has certainly evolved." I guess it has. Over the years, I've had the privilege of writing on a subject I love, coaching hundreds of different people, and speaking to thousands more. Over my many years as a writer, speaker, and facilitator, I have discovered a commonality in our human experience: the desire to be all we can be – to reach our full potential – to put our gifts and talents to good use.

The great motivator Brian Tracy once said, "Successful people are always looking for opportunities to help others. Unsuccessful people are always asking, 'What's in it for me?'" When we extend our hand, it should always be as an offer to help.

Though our life experience is uniquely ours, we humans often find ourselves in similar situations in search of answers to the same questions. Perhaps by sharing our journey we can help each other to arrive at that place of understanding and enlightenment.

"Man is eminently a storyteller. His search for a purpose, a cause, an ideal, a mission, and the like is largely a search for a plot and a pattern in the development of his life story – a story that is basically without meaning or pattern."

– Eric Hoffer, American writer

Section One:
Two Steps Back

"And since you know you cannot see yourself, so well as by reflection, I, your glass, will modestly discover to yourself, that of yourself which you yet know not of."

– William Shakespeare

"Am I simply the product of my genetics, upbringing, personal history, and beliefs? Partially, but when the rest is stripped away, who am I at my core? Here lies the key to my achievements, successes, the impact I will have, and my sense of fulfillment."

– Murray Fuhrer, *Extreme Esteem*

Factor Number One:
Early Programming

"What the hell were you thinking?" snarled the older man.

Tears welled up in the little boy's eyes.

"Dry up!" spat the man. "Don't you start blubbering now!"

The boy tried in vain to fight back the sobs that began to rack his body.

"I pity you, boy," said the man, shaking his head. "Life's gonna be hell!"

For the little boy, his father's words became prophetic.

Early childhood experiences can have a tremendous impact upon our self-esteem. If positive, the experiences inspire and empower us, preparing us to act decisively and deal effectively with life's challenges. If negative, the experience can leave us feeling defeated, powerless, and inadequate.

Practitioners of self-esteem and empowerment training refer to these experiences as early programming. The term is apt, as these experiences become the foundation upon which you build your life. They also become the standard or filter through which all subsequent experiences are viewed and evaluated.

If you were repeatedly told as a child that you were smart, creative, and capable, chances are you'd view yourself and the world in a far different manner than the child who was told he was stupid, dense, and good for nothing.

Certainly, the temperament of the individual plays a role in the long-term effects of early programming. While some people are devastated by the experiences of youth, others rise above their early programming or even use it as a source of inspiration.

Such was the case with a man I met who grew up with an abusive, alcoholic father. Now a successful leader in his community, this man has often stated, "My father was the best negative role model I could ever have. I learned at a young age how *not* to live my life."

Sadly, that's not the way things work out for most people. Here's part of the reason: an estimated 80 percent of our belief system is in place by the time we're 10 years old and only 10 percent of us will ever raise our awareness and re-examine those beliefs.

You've heard of Mustard Seed Faith, as in, "If you have faith as small as a mustard seed, you can move mountains. Nothing will be impossible for you."

For the most part, your life is a reflection of where you've placed your faith. I'm not speaking in religious terms here, but rather about what you hold fundamentally true for you. If you've invested your faith in a set of well-considered and positive beliefs, you will accomplish great feats – you will move mountains. If your faith is misplaced – if you have invested heavily in a set of false or self-defeating beliefs – then your faith will bring into your life a series of failures, dashed hopes, and heartaches.

Understand now, the same mechanism is at play; the same unstoppable force has been put into motion. It is simply the manifestation or the results of that faith that are different. This investment often happens at an unconscious level, out of reach of our conscious awareness.

You see, lack of awareness is the same as having no choice. Most people never raise their awareness to the point of recognizing and releasing poor early programming. You are not among that group; the very fact you're reading these words is proof of such.

As you become awake and aware of all life holds for you, you'll need to make a choice: to stay with your inner discomfort and current belief system or to walk clear of it. I think you'll walk clear.

Two Questions

"All men should strive to learn before they die what they are running from, and to, and why."

– James Thurber, author, cartoonist, and humorist

Are you stuck? Do you find that despite all the passion you put into your own personal development, despite all the tools you've acquired, the courses you've taken, the books you've read, that you are still stuck in some aspect of your work, life, or relationships?

If this were an advertisement for almost any personal development program, I would now be telling you that I had found the one perfect technique that makes all the others obsolete. The one secret that will finally get you everything you desire and deserve. I won't do that because I don't think there is one all encompassing secret, technique, or technology out there. The truth is I am stuck occasionally too, in my business, in a relationship, in my personal development. I go back to two basic questions: "Who am I?" and "How will I live my life?" These two questions underpin every spiritual quest.

Am I simply the product of my genetics, upbringing, personal history, and beliefs? Partially, but when the rest is stripped away, who am I at my core? Here lies the key to my achievements, successes, the impact I will have, and my sense of fulfillment.

For me, the best way to get close to "Who Am I?" is through the practice of quieting the mind. In essence, by becoming still, silent, and willing to reject my habitual need to define who I am by what I do. I may be a writer, a motivational speaker, a business owner, but that's what I do, it is *not* who I am. It's easy to confuse the two, yet vital to draw a distinction. If I am what I do, then what happens to me when I'm no longer able to do it? If I tie my sense of self directly to my occupation, I run the risk of losing myself should I lose my occupation (which often happens when people retire!).

The only way to know who I am is to spend time being alone with myself. No distractions, no temptations, no desires, none of the tyranny of the ever active, noisy mind. Thinking about my desires just tells me what I want. Thinking about what society requires, what responsibility demands, or what I need to do to achieve my desires just tells me about how I move toward desires or away from fears. Sitting and finding the still point is how I find myself and discover who I really am.

Asking, "How will I live my life?" challenges me to bring more of myself into my life – into my relationships, my work, into how I express my purpose. This question helps me make the right judgments about whom I want to be with, where I want to work, whom I want to engage with socially. When I ask this question at a deep level, I get a different set of answers to questions like, "What do I wish to possess?" "What do I want to achieve?" or "What must I do?" This question becomes, "How will I bring my heart, my spirit, my soul fully into the world so that it is visible, active, engaged with vitality?"

When the answers to these questions start to align, then and only then do I know who I really am and how I will live my life. Only then, am I being deeply authentic, living my life on purpose, and bringing my purpose to life.

It's Time to Wake Up

"A lie, told often enough, becomes the truth."

– V.I. Lenin, founder of the Russian Communist Party and leader of the Russian Revolution.

The other day someone used the term "conscious sleep." They were speaking of lucid dreaming: the ability some people have to be consciously aware while dreaming. The term conscious sleep could easily apply to the state many of us are in each day. Eyes open, body in motion, yet asleep – oblivious to the big picture, the endless possibilities.

The truth is life can be so much better than we have it! We seldom come to that realization, so that's not the way it turns out for most of us. Instead of enjoying the life we want, most of us wind up enduring an existence that's tolerable at best.

And we do it – and continue to do it – because most of us have been brainwashed into believing life is "supposed" to be hard, a struggle – so that's the way we make it.

Where did we get such an idea? It was pounded into our heads from the moment we were born as the "right way" to live, and we bought it all without question. Almost immediately the "big people" in our lives and the institutions of whatever culture we were born into began "teaching" us all the "right" beliefs, attitudes, values, fears, and behaviors (or at least what they believed was right).

So what happened? We were lulled into conscious sleep by a bunch of old ideas – old ways of thinking and being that are now keeping us from getting what we want. And get this: 80 percent of those ideas were locked into our heads by the time we were 10 years old, and 90 percent of us never change them.

So it's no wonder we make some poor, self-defeating choices: our belief system constantly filters all incoming data and screens out everything that doesn't fit with what we "know" to be true. It's hard to wake up and see, often for the first time, who we are and what's really happening to us – hard to question everything we've been told and believed, from the most sacred to the most profane.

But, once we wake up, an amazing thing happens. No longer willing to blindly accept the teachings, rants, and preachings of others, we begin searching for what's true for us. And watch the reaction of those around you – arms flailing, eyes bulging, voices cracking, they break into a rant: "All you care about is yourself! Just who do you think you are? What would happen if everybody lived like that!"

If you're up for a little fun, smile and answer, "They'd all be happy!"

You see, lack of awareness – conscious sleep – is the same as having no choice. As you begin to raise your level of awareness and acknowledge the fact that life is filled with possibilities, you'll have a choice to make. To stay stuck and in pain – the victim of a self-defeating set of beliefs or to stand up and yell, "No, I'm not going to take it anymore!" I chose to stand up and I think you'll do exactly the same thing.

At some point we all need to ask, "Which do I want: prison or freedom?" Wake up and unlock the door to your personal freedom. You were born to succeed – to be happy. Only you can claim your rightful inheritance. The choice is yours no matter what your age. You and you alone create your world. If you vote to open your eyes, nothing can hold you back.

Let Go of the Penny

"The further behind I leave the past, the closer I am to forging my own character."

– Isabelle Eberhardt, explorer

Once upon a time, a little boy got his hand stuck in the neck of a valuable antique vase. His parents tried twisting and turning the vase, pulling and tugging, even pouring oil into the mouth of the vase – all in a futile attempt to slide his hand out. Finally, just as they were resigned to breaking the vase to rescue the frightened child, his mother said, "Now, Billy, let's try one more time. Keep your fingers straight, tuck in your thumb, and relax while Mommy pulls on the vase." To this, Billy replied, "Mommy, I can't do that! If I open my fingers, I'll drop my penny!"

What "pennies" are you holding onto – old ideas or false beliefs held so tightly in your grip that they're keeping you stuck in your current situation, keeping you from being as happy or successful as your desires and capabilities would allow you to be? Most of us don't even realize we're hanging on tight to false or outdated ideas and that certain aspects of our existence are being controlled by an old belief system.

Talk to most people and it's like swimming up to a talking fish (you'll have to use your imagination) and asking the fish, "What's it like to live in the water?"

"Water?" the fish replies, "What's water?" It doesn't know that "water" exists or that "water" is controlling its life. The same thing happens with most of us everyday.

Though our self-limiting beliefs may not be immediately apparent to us, we can spot them by following the thread back from the current difficulties they are causing in our life. Ask yourself what beliefs you are holding onto about yourself, others, and the world that are bringing you an unwelcome response. For instance, let's say you have an eating disorder and go on a binge whenever you feel anxious. This difficulty might then be traced to a belief you accepted while young that eating makes everything OK. An unexamined belief will continue to inspire behavior even though it is no longer – as in the above example – relieving the anxiety. Once you identify the belief or cluster of beliefs, and you can see how it's no longer delivering the desire you want, you can begin to put into place healthier, more productive beliefs that will support your growth.

Most of us received a lot more negative programming than positive in our childhood. You may have been told you weren't very good at something, that you'd never make a living if you chose a certain career path, or that you'd never get a good job if you didn't go to college. As if all that wasn't enough, you managed to impose your own self-limiting beliefs on yourself as well. You may have taken on the belief that you're too fat, tall, dumb, skinny, or uneducated to pursue and actually accomplish your dreams.

Beliefs are a crucial factor to success in life, so we must learn to rid ourselves of the negative, self-limiting ones and create positive, self-enabling beliefs. Remember: past programming created our belief system, our beliefs guide our actions, and our actions create our reality, so it makes sense to rid ourselves of negative programming.

Are you stuck holding on tightly to self-limiting beliefs? Let go and believe that you can do anything and have anything you want, and then watch your life change!

Flying on Autopilot

"Plant the seeds of failure and failure will follow. And since the only real freedom a person has is the choice of what thoughts he will feed to his Inner-Consciousness, he is totally responsible for the outcomes he gets."

– Sidney Madwed, writer, speaker, motivator

There are modern autopilots that can land an airplane in zero visibility. Most of the older systems require the pilot to disconnect at about 200 feet above the ground and manually land the airplane. Pilots like to fly airplanes, so unless the autopilot is required they prefer to switch off the system, grasp the controls firmly with both hands and take charge of the aircraft.

It's the same with life. Fundamental change requires that you switch off the autopilot. Many of us think we're "doing our own thing" when we're literally captives of our past – living life on autopilot. Daily we grind out self-defeating choices that entrap us. Our past programming controls us. Our lives are predictably monotonous round trips, not adventurous journeys.

Early in life, Dwayne (not his real name) concluded he was a failure. His father had told him so since he was a child. Despite his best efforts, Dwayne could never win his father's approval. Dwayne worked hard to build the family business and was the obvious choice to take over the reins. Instead, when his father retired he signed over all assets to Dwayne's irresponsible, less competent brother. Shortly after, Dwayne's father died and the business faltered. Although extremely bright and competent, Dwayne had difficulty working for other people and never stayed at any one job for long. Eventually, Dwayne set up his own business at enormous financial sacrifice. Just as the fledgling operation began to make money, he sold it at a loss. Reluctantly, Dwayne went back working for someone else.

Vocationally, financially and emotionally Dwayne's old programming directed all his choices. He allowed his past conditioning to rule his life. Dwayne was flying on autopilot. He consistently and mechanically avoided solutions that would work in his favor. Why? In order to maintain a familiar climate of pain, failure, and abandonment.

The problem is that long after we leave the influence of those who programmed us (they may even be dead), we keep their instructions ruling our lives. Originally, we were influenced by their voice and modeling. Then through lack of awareness, we kept re-indoctrinating ourselves by playing their words in our heads. Once they made us feel "bad." Now we take over the job by parenting ourselves with their phantom talk. Today's pain comes from imitating voices from your past. To increase your self-esteem you need to change your belief system about yourself.

Start by putting each belief about yourself through a special "litmus" test. This simple, yet powerful test has helped many people take that first all-important step toward self-awareness and enlightenment. Ask yourself, "Is this belief a fact? Does it serve my best interest? Does it advance or protect my health? Does it get me what I want, need, or deserve?" Chances are many of your self-beliefs will fail the litmus test. If they fail, discard them and form a new and healthier version.

The basic issue is not what happened in the past, but rather what you choose to hold true for yourself today. Will you choose to be a slave to old programming and child-born illusions, bound by an inappropriate and worn-out belief system? Changing those beliefs doesn't happen overnight, it's a process, which begins with awareness – so switch off autopilot, grasp the controls firmly with both hands, and take charge of your life.

Secondary Gain

n. Interpersonal or social advantages gained indirectly from organic illness, such as an increase in attention from others.

– The American Heritage Stedman's Medical Dictionary

There's a saying about success in life or anything else for that matter: "Many of us don't want to admit that we've been standing in our own way." Allow me to explain. Let's say you've been working hard to move beyond a certain issue – affirming, visualizing, and meditating – but you can't seem to move beyond a certain belief or behavior. You may be dealing with secondary gain.

Secondary gain is a psychiatric term meaning that a person has a hidden reason for holding onto an undesirable habit, belief, or condition. People with secondary gain issues hang on tight to negative beliefs or behaviors because (at a subconscious level) there's a payoff – a benefit to maintaining the old ways of thinking and doing. For example, you may have a great entrepreneurial idea – a real winner. You're committed to quitting your secure, full-time job and pursuing your dream once your bills are down to a manageable level, but that level is never attained. In fact, the more you focus on the new idea, the more your debt load seems to grow. Recognize the secondary gain? The ever-growing debt prevents you from putting yourself out there – from facing your fear of risking or losing your safe, secure source of income. Once you recognize secondary gain, you can find alternative ways to fulfill your desires.

What can trigger a secondary gain issue? Let's consider the most common culprits.

Fear of responsibility. Perhaps you feel added success, love, or prosperity will demand more than you can provide. You may be exposed as a fraud – "found out" as not being truly capable or deserving of this higher level of good.

Loss of love. If you change too much, you may move out of the sphere of your current peer group, family, friends, or romantic relationship.

Loss of consideration. Ironically, some people will hang onto a painful condition because they desire the sympathy and allowances others make because of their suffering.

If you're getting an emotional reaction from reading this – anger, loss, or frustration – *this is your own secondary gain issue coming up*. You may be getting hints of it right now. If so, write them down. Like a mouse in the house, it will try to hide from your conscious detection. Writing it down will hold it in conscious awareness. You can also try talking to a friend or speaking into a tape recorder. Start coming up with ideas of what your secondary gain might be. Speculate. If you catch a glimpse of what it actually is, write it down. An excellent way of viewing this is to ask, "What good reason do I have for keeping this habit or belief – for not allowing my dreams to materialize?"

Get the reason(s) on paper or tape. There may be more than one. Perhaps the whole idea of creating a new and better life is a little frightening. Once you unearth the issue, go to work on it. For additional encouragement, join a support group, journal on it, meditate about it, do all the things you would do to heal a conscious issue. Owning up to a secondary gain issue doesn't make you a bad person. On the contrary, it shows the world that you are a courageous and aware individual, willing to face the truth that lies within.

Validation

"Praise is like sunlight to the human spirit: we cannot flower and grow without it."

– Jess Lair, PhD, author of *I Ain't Much, Baby, But I'm All I've Got*

We all need time and room to think, people to hug, friends who make us laugh, enough discomfort to give us cause to reflect, and enough comfort to help us feel we belong, we matter, we are valued and validated in our work place, homes, and community.

Validation lets other people know we hold them in esteem – that we are paying attention to the verbal and non-verbal messages they send and we want to understand the feelings behind their words and stories. Validating sends a message that we want to make a connection of the heart as well as the head. Validations help to build bridges, connect at deeper emotional levels, and to develop healthy, accepting, and affirming relationships.

Here's a wonderful story about validation gleaned from *Prescription for Peace*, the ever-popular empowerment book by Steve Goodier. Goodier explains how a simple ball of yarn became a web of love for a teacher and one classroom of high school students.

"Their teacher seated the students in a circle on the carpeted floor. One member of the group was instructed to toss a ball of yarn to someone across the circle, holding tightly to one end. The recipient took hold of the string and listened as the one who tossed it shared something that she especially liked about him. Keeping hold of the string, he then tossed the ball across the circle to someone else and affirmed something positive about her. The ball of yarn was tossed across and around the circle until everyone had both heard and shared encouragement. The yarn became a woven web of love and good feelings.

"Before they went their separate ways, the teacher took scissors and snipped through the web. Each person took a piece of yarn away as a remembrance of the special words he or she had heard. Many of them wore cherished pieces of yarn around their wrists for days and weeks afterward."

This aptly demonstrates how much validation means to most people. Although it would be unrealistic and unnecessary to validate someone all the time every time, we can certainly avoid invalidating him or her. Invalidating people involves treating them as if they are less: less important, less intelligent, less valued, less appreciated and less worthy. It may not be conscious and it may be done with positive intent, but when it is done, invalidating chips away at the very essence of an individual's sense of self and diminishes his or her self-esteem.

If you don't notice or can't think of something positive to say, or if you don't have enough energy to offer something appreciative, find the strength and wisdom not to make a hurtful, hateful, or unkind remark. Such behavior may put down the other person, but it also demeans the one who does it. If you chip away at someone's heart for long enough, that heart just may withdraw to the point where it no longer allows validation, appreciation, or even love to enter.

Validation is one of the keys to nurturing an open heart, so always give three times as much praise and validation as criticism. Find opportunities to affirm others throughout the day. Few people grow weary of hearing sincere admiration and praise. And each time you give it, you help to create an invisible web of love that can last a lifetime.

The Power of Touch

"It is the magic of a touch, the power of a hug that makes life joyful."

– Dr. Michael G. Rayel, author, psychiatrist, and inventor

The other day, I came across a disturbing statistic: a century ago, the majority of babies in American orphanages died before the age of seven months. At the time, orphanages were an everyday part of the social landscape. Despite modern antiseptic procedures and adequate food, the mortality rate among these discarded children was heartbreaking. The babies died not from infectious diseases or malnutrition, but from a lack of human contact – touch. Sterile surroundings could not prevent it and having enough food made no difference. When the babies were placed in environments where they received physical nurturing, love and attention, they gained weight and ultimately flourished.

A recent study suggests that children welcomed with physical touch and tactile stimulation grow into well-adjusted, capable and loving adults. These children enjoy lower anxiety levels, fewer symptoms of depression, and improved self-esteem. Children deprived of touch in infancy show tendencies toward aggressiveness and violent behavior.

Unquestionably, touch is vital for infant survival, but equally vital to the emotional well-being of growing children and adults. Some time ago, I attended a personal empowerment workshop. The facilitator, a registered massage therapist, talked about the healing power of touch and encouraged everyone to share a hug with his or her partner. One of the participants was a spirited 83-year-old man. His partner, a gregarious young woman said, "Come here, you!" and gave him a huge "bear like" hug. The older man began sobbing uncontrollably – tears rolled unabashed down his cheeks. "What's wrong?" asked the young woman. Between sobs, the old man explained that was the first time anyone had hugged or held him in over 20 years. We were all affected by the magnitude of the admission. Touch deprivation is real for many people.

Why is touch so powerful? What magical events transpire when skin contacts skin? And what is the connection between physical human contact and virtually every aspect of health and well-being? The sensation of touch begins in the womb. The skin, derived from the same cells as the nervous system, is a perfect instrument for collecting information about our environment long before birth. A fetus will withdraw from the touch of a probe at less than eight weeks of gestation, showing that the link between touch and survival is one of the first and most important protective mechanisms to develop.

A touch provides comfort in a cold world. It makes us feel secure – uniting us with an affectionate, loving, and feeling human being. The warmth it brings is better than the warmth of a fireplace. A touch shields us from the worries of today and delivers a tangible boost in self-confidence. Like the Internet, it allows high-speed access to another soul.

As we grow, our need for touch does not disappear. When my wife hugs me at night, I can feel all my aches and concerns of the day disappear. When I come home after a full day's work and my kids hug me, I feel an immediate rejuvenation – stress melts away and I'm filled with joy and hope. We continue to benefit from the touch we receive from those who love and care for us. Make a point to include more nurturing touch in your life and in the lives of infants, children, teenagers, spouses, and elderly family members.

Heal From the Inside Out

"Without a humble but reasonable confidence in your own powers you cannot be successful or happy."

– Norman Vincent Peale, founder of the Positive Thinking Foundation and Guideposts

Ever had an issue in your life that just wouldn't go away? It might be weight, abundance, health, or some other problem that just wouldn't improve no matter how hard you focused on it. The fact is, many of us try to change our lives by working on the symptoms rather than the issues. It's kind of like working to dispel the smoke without putting out the fire. "OK, I need to lose a few pounds. I'll just diet and exercise." We lose the weight, but within a short time, the pounds are back and they've brought along a few friends.

Some people who have been overweight most of their lives have a tough time adjusting to being slim after they've released the excess pounds. They may still have a self-image of being overweight, and that must change before the weight reduction can be permanent. You may have a belief that you're not worthy of success or happiness and that influences any attempt to create a better life. It causes you to hold yourself back or sabotage your progress. All of these notions and many others could simply be outdated beliefs that have operated below your mental radar and now keep you from the life you deserve.

Dealing only with symptoms moves us from one quick fix to another, often only perpetuating the problem. An old adage says, "Those who don't learn from their history are doomed to repeat it." Twelve-step recovery programs are frequently built upon this concept and members are counseled to heal old wounds before starting new relationships.

A friend of mine recently left one job where he felt unappreciated for another job where he felt certain his new boss would recognize his talents and treat him with approval and respect. Moreover, for a short time, his new employer did treat him well, but after a time and a number of recurring problems, he began treating him in the same manner as his original employer. Since my friend hadn't dealt with the underlying issues, they quickly returned.

Symptoms can be the outward manifestation of an idea held deep within your subconscious mind – an idea formed as a child and one that you've lived with for so long now that it has become an unconscious pattern. For example, you might have imposed an unconscious limit to your income and you're holding tight to an image of yourself as broke.

Doctors will tell us a physical wound has to heal from the inside out. It's the same with internal issues. There are many ways to heal the inner wounds. Start by being completely honest with yourself and objective. Assess what image you may be holding of yourself or about the issue, and work toward changing that image to reflect your desired outcome. Examine your attitudes about the change you want. Write down everything you think and say about your goal. Journal about it, asking what could be blocking you.

Often – at some level – we're aware of our issues; we simply choose to keep them from the light. It's hard to work in the dark. But unless you deal with the underlying cause of the issue, it will continue to reassert itself, and more aggressively with each reemergence. You and I are only limited by our efforts and faith! Believe in yourself!

Tangled Cords

"The outer conditions of a person's life will always be found to reflect their inner beliefs."

– James Lane Allen, the Kentucky Schoolmaster

I don't know about you, but I believe the cables and cords that run to and from computers have lives of their own. Have you ever untangled all the cables and cords only to find that within a few days they have retangled themselves?

Have you ever noticed that some people are walking bundles of tangled cords? We all have beliefs and habits that sometimes seem to conflict. When these conflicting beliefs get in the way of achieving goals, it's time to re-examine and change them. One pitfall is that sometimes we don't even know that our beliefs are limiting us!

Creating your own reality is a little more complicated than saying, "I choose this, I choose that, I believe this, I believe that," and instantly you have a healthy relationship, financial security, a better job, and more intimate friendships. You may have already tried talking yourself into new choices and beliefs only to run into a wall – a seemingly insurmountable block that despite your best efforts forced you back into the box. That wall, that seemingly insurmountable block, is your subconscious. The reason your old choices and beliefs continue to rear their ugly heads is deep in your subconscious mind you have conflicting beliefs regarding your ability to succeed, to become wealthy, to lose weight, to be confident, to find your soul mate. Until you challenge those pre-existing beliefs, you will find permanent change difficult or even impossible to attain.

Conflicting beliefs create an internal "tug-of-war" between our desire to do something and feeling as though we can't or shouldn't do it. How do you know if your beliefs are in conflict? Is procrastination a regular part of your day? Do you have a difficult time getting motivated to do the things you really want to do? Did you tell yourself that this would be your year to succeed, but despite this promise to yourself, you're still not living the life you truly want to live? Do people often misunderstand your intentions?

You may not even realize that old and outdated beliefs are still in play. Watch for times when you feel challenged or pressured to perform and listen to the statements you make at that point. Many beliefs we hold onto no longer benefit us; these statements will provide an insight into our current belief system. "I can't speak in front of a group," or, "I don't work well under pressure," or, "I've tried to quit (a habit) but I just can't do it." Do these statements have any basis in reality? Put them through the litmus test for beliefs and find out.

Here's how it works. Let's take the statement, "I can't speak in front of a group." Test it for validity by honestly answering the question, "Is it a true statement or someone's opinion?" Make note of the answer. Second question: "Does this belief help me learn, grow, and succeed?" Again, note the answer. Finally, ask the question, "What good reason do I have for keeping this belief?" Make note of the answer. If your belief fails the litmus test (and most conflicting beliefs do) then discard it.

Do the mental cables and cords tangle again? You had better believe they do! The difference is that now – thanks to a higher level of understanding – you can untangle them again!

Every Word Counts

"Kind words can be short and easy to speak, but their echoes are truly endless."

– Mother Theresa

"This is Jimmy," announced the teacher. "He's just moved here with his family from Saskatchewan."

Jimmy had a predominant overbite and the thick lenses in his glasses made his blue eyes appear enormous.

"I know you'll all make Jimmy feel welcome in his new school."

Jimmy looked up nervously and smiled. Some of the students smiled back, some stared blankly at the outsider. One loud voice in the back of the room yelled, "I've never seen a four-eyed gopher before!"

Laughter erupted. The teacher quickly silenced the group, chastised the heckler, and apologized for the comment. Jimmy's face was red as he dropped into his desk. The few snickers that rippled through the room were quickly shushed and I watched as Jimmy slowly crumpled from sight.

As years wore on, the kid in the back of the classroom most likely forgot the entire episode. He was never aware of the pain he inflicted on sensitive, insecure 12-year-old Jimmy. I can tell you one thing: Jimmy never forgot. His self-image and self-esteem had taken a direct hit and the damage was devastating.

Our words can be empowering and uplifting or critical and injurious. Words can either help or hurt us; words can add to or take away from someone else.

Educator and writer Leo Buscaglia put it like this: "The majority of us lead quiet, unheralded lives as we pass through this world. There will most likely be no tickertape parades for us, no monuments created in our honour. But that does not lessen our possible impact, for there are scores of people waiting for someone just like us to come along; people who will appreciate our compassion, our encouragement, who will need our unique talents. Someone who will live a happier life merely because we took the time to share what we had to give. Too often we underestimate the power of a touch, a smile, a kind word, a listening ear, an honest compliment, or the smallest act of caring, all of which have the potential to turn a life around. It's overwhelming to consider the continuous opportunities there are to make our love felt."

We've all been raised with the phrase, "Sticks and stones may break my bones but names will never hurt me." In fact, names do hurt. Words hurt – especially cruel words. Many of us have been on the receiving end and, chances are, we've done some giving, too. Certainly, all of us have witnessed cruel and unkind comments made to others.

Some comments are blatantly cruel, while others take the form of sarcastic remarks. I'm not speaking of good-natured teasing – though that too can cross the line. Sarcastic remarks may appear harmless, yet can be equally demoralizing. Cruel comments and sarcastic remarks can leave the giver and the receiver feeling negative and critical. Along with harsh words come unpleasant feelings, such as anger, sadness, and regret.

The reverse is also true. When we speak kindly of others it focuses our attention on their goodness. When we speak kindly of our circumstances it turns our thoughts from envy to gratitude. Kind words have the power to heal and to lift. Speaking kindly shows that we care about the person to whom we're speaking. We all feel good when we say kind words to others and when kind words are spoken to us.

For the sake of your own self-esteem, it's important to let others know immediately if their words are hurtful or inappropriate. I wish I could say that Jimmy eventually recovered his sense of self-worth, but I can't. When I last saw Jimmy – some years ago – he was still self-conscious, a little bitter, and occasionally very angry.

My mother used to say, "If you can't say something nice, don't say anything at all." Good advice – then and now.

Keep Believing in Yourself

"Nobody will believe in you unless you believe in yourself."

– Liberace, pianist

Harvey Mackay, business motivational speaker and *New York Times* bestselling author of *Beware the Naked Man Who Offers You His Shirt*, tells an insightful story about a professor and a class of 30 senior molecular biology students. The professor was about to pass out the final exam.

"I have been privileged to be your instructor this semester," he said, "and I know how hard you have all worked to prepare for this test. I also know most of you are off to medical school or graduate school next fall. I am well aware of how much pressure you are under to keep your GPAs up, and because I know you are all capable of understanding this material, I am prepared to offer an automatic B to anyone who would prefer not to take the final."

The relief was palpable as a number of students jumped up, thanked the professor and left the class. The professor looked at the handful of students who remained, and offered again, "Any other takers?" One more student decided to leave.

Seven students remained. The professor closed the door and took attendance. Then he handed out the final exam. There were two sentences typed on the paper: "Congratulations, you have just received an A in this class. Keep believing in yourself."

The same is true for students of life. The A students are those who believe in what they're doing because they've learned from both successes and failures. They've assimilated life's lessons, whether from formal education or the school of life, and become better, stronger people.

Psychologists estimate that by the age of two, 50 percent of what we ever believe about ourselves has been formed; by age six, 60 percent; by ten years, 80 percent. Have you ever longed for the energy and optimism of a child? Everything is possible – there is nothing you can't do, learn, or be. However, you're no longer a child, and you realize you have some limits. Don't let your biggest limitation be you.

Take your cue from Sir Edmund Hillary, the first person to reach the summit of Mount Everest. When asked about the feat, Hillary replied, "It's not the mountain we conquer, but ourselves." Believing in yourself comes from knowing what you are capable of doing and doing it well. It also means realizing that you're not going to succeed every time. Baseball great Mickey Mantle struck out more than 1,700 times, but it didn't stop him from becoming a legendary ball player. He believed in himself, and he knew his fans believed in him.

So, how do you nurture a strong belief in yourself? Never stop learning! Don't limit yourself only to job-related classes, either. Learn as much as you can about every subject that interests you. When you know what you're talking about, it shows.

Never confuse confidence with an over-sized ego. If you want people to believe in you, you must also believe in them. Those around you have much to contribute, and they deserve your support. Without faith in yourself and others, success is impossible.

Surround yourself with positive people! Positive people understand the importance of self-belief. They will help you keep focused on what you can do rather than what you can't. Remember: you become whom you surround yourself with. Whom have you chosen?

You Belong to the Sky

"A strong, positive self-image is the best possible preparation for success."

– Dr. Joyce Brothers, psychologist, columnist, author and business consultant

One day, while walking in the woods, a farmer found an unusual egg on the ground and placed it gently in the breast pocket of his coveralls. When he got home, he showed the egg to his wife, who suggested he put it in the nest of a brood hen. The man felt certain the egg would never hatch, but placed it under the hen, nonetheless. The egg did hatch and the mother hen cared for the awkward chick as though it were one of her own.

Over time, the chick grew into a healthy, young eagle. The eagle matured with the chickens and enjoyed a quiet life on the farm. The farmer and his wife marveled at how the eagle scratched the earth for worms and seeds. How he clucked and cackled. And, most amazingly, how – when he thrashed his wings – he could fly only a few feet into the air. The eagle did what the barnyard chickens did, believing he was a barnyard chicken.

Years passed and the eagle grew old. One day he saw a magnificent bird circling overhead in a blue and cloudless sky. It glided in graceful majesty, lifted by the mighty wind currents, with scarcely a beat of its powerful, golden wings.

The old eagle stared heavenward in awe. "Who's that?" he asked. "That's the eagle, the King of Birds," said one of the chickens. "He belongs to the sky. We belong to the earth." So the eagle lived and died a chicken, wishing he had been born an eagle.

This story reminds us how important a healthy self-image is and how inaccurate our own self-image may be. A good self-image allows you to see yourself as a unique and significant person – one who has a meaningful part to play in the world. A poor self-image can be an invisible ceiling and prevent you from enjoying success and reaching your true potential. Here are some tips to build and enjoy a healthy self-image.

Enjoy Who You Are. The way you laugh and smile, the way you view the world, the way you think, are all uniquely yours. Acknowledge the whole you, not just your body.

Accept Yourself As You Are. Accept who you are as you are right now while preparing and planning for change and growth in the future.

Recognize Your Worth. Try this exercise. Make a list of 50 things you have accomplished in your life. Consider your entire life. You will be surprised at how many things, small and big, you can add to the list. You may find that despite past mistakes or problems, you deserve a pat on the back for the good that you have done.

Be Kind to Yourself. No matter what people say to us, the things we say to ourselves are much worse and do far more damage. Focus on your successes and don't dwell on your mistakes or failures. Many of the things that contribute to an individual's poor self-image are relics of the past. It is never too late to release the past and start anew.

Cultivating a positive self-image can help add greater meaning and purpose to your life. Remember, you are a unique and significant person – one who has a meaningful part to play in the world. You belong to the sky.

Factor Number One Summary:
Early Programing

Early programming beliefs are something we accept as true, without question. We live our life around them, often without thinking about them, questioning them or even being aware of them. An estimated 80 percent of our belief system is in place by the time we're 10 years old and only 10 percent of us will ever raise our awareness and re-examine those beliefs. Lack of awareness is the same as having no choice at all.

Here are some questions pertaining to negative early programming that you may wish to ponder by yourself or discuss as a group.

1. Can I trace a self-defeating belief about myself back to a childhood experience?
2. Do I become angry and defensive when someone challenges my opinion?
3. Do I have difficulty supporting my opinion or position?
4. Am I often dealing with issues of deservability or lack of self-worth?
5. Does the voice of my inner critic often become loud and condemning?
6. Do I often feel like a child again when dealing with criticism?
7. Of the two principal motivating emotions – fear and love – which (most often) directs my choices in life?
8. How long does it take me to recover from emotional upset in my life?

Factor Number Two: Reinforcement of Belief

Noted American author, Brenda Hammond wrote seven of the most profound words I have ever read. They read as such: "If fear alters behavior, you're already defeated."

The other day my friend Lynn and I were talking about repetitive patterns of behavior. We've all been there at one time or another: despite our best efforts, finding ourselves repeatedly in the same kind of unhealthy relationship or stressful financial situations. Lynn made the comment, "It's no fun being stuck in the spin cycle."

I thought her choice of the phrase "spin cycle" was appropriate. Forever tumbling in turmoil, unable to break free of a patently destructive pattern of behavior. Our seeming inability to resolve these patterns can be demoralizing and affect our sense of self-worth.

If you find yourself standing at the crossroads and forever choosing the same path, it's time to raise your awareness, and the first step is to take notice. Take a good, long look at your life and try to notice repeating patterns. As best you can, move your point of consciousness around to that of an objective observer. Watch your interactions with others.

As you scan for recurring themes, notice when certain interactions made you feel angry, sad, rejected, or frightened. Virtually any emotion you haven't released will manifest some place in your body. Watch for tension spots in your neck, back, or forehead. Stomach problems, loss of appetite, or poor digestion are all indicators of "held" pain.

Once you unearth a pattern (generally, a couple will immediately surface) and decide you want to heal it, the first challenge you'll probably meet is resistance. Resistance is actually an automatic survival mechanism. Use the presence of fear and resistance as an indicator that you've unearthed a pattern truly worth exploring and resolving.

The first step in shifting any long-standing pattern of behavior is to make new and better choices. Let's say you're at the mall and spy a great special on jeans. Instantly, you reach for your credit card. Perhaps, amassing staggering credit card debts has been a recurring theme for you. As you stand there with "plastic" in your hand, consider yourself at the crossroads. Instead of rushing headlong into the fitting room, try staying quiet and sensing how you feel. Rather than submitting to the urge, try saying "no" to it.

Initially, it may seem as though you're only pretending things have changed when, at the point your old behavior asserts itself, you make a different choice. However, if you let yourself move far enough into this "pretending" process, you'll disrupt the old pattern, create a new neural pathway, and lay the foundation for more positive life experiences.

When you begin to challenge old patterns, you may find repressed emotions such as fear, anger, or regret rising to the surface of your conscious awareness. While in this disrupted, temporarily unfrozen state, allow any pain associated with those old patterns to be expressed. If you find yourself releasing a good deal of negative emotion at this point, it's a good sign you're making progress.

There is a natural ebb and flow through resolving old patterning: noticing, sensing, consciously opposing the pattern and expressing the pain. Seldom does breaking a pattern occur the first time. Be gentle and forgiving with yourself during this process.

It's a wonderful moment when you feel the pattern break and experience freedom. You stop responding to old programming or knee-jerk into an old pattern. You have the freedom to choose a new response – to come up with fresh and creative ways to deal with situations that you may never have considered before. The "spin cycle" is over.

Casting Off

"As a teacher, I often sense the presence of something transcendent – a spiritual electricity, if you will – and I have come to rely on it in transcending my own limitations."

– Julia Cameron, author of *The Artist's Way*

"Do you really need all those books?" My wife has been helping me move into my new home office. She's helping me *not* take the clutter of my current office into my new space. I admit it: I love books and I have hundreds.

One of those books is *The Artist's Way* by Julia Cameron. It's about awakening and nurturing creativity in all its forms. (Julia explains, making a great soup is as much of a creative expression as creating a great painting.) What struck me most was her description of how non-artists misunderstand the nature of creativity. Non-artists look at creative people (musicians, painters, sculptures, writers, and such) with envy, believing the artist possesses something they don't. "He's such a great musician. I have no talent whatsoever," or, "She's such a fantastic writer. Wish I had been born with her gift." However, there's a false assumption at play here. According to Cameron, artists don't have something the rest of the world lacks – rather, they have removed barriers to the natural creativity that's available to all of us. Artists don't have something extra, the rest of the world does: self-limiting beliefs.

I believe the same is true when it comes to self-esteem. For years I've watched good people struggle, believing that if only they had the right tools or had been born with the gift of self-assurance, they could live confidently and energetically. They spend years going to classes and coaches, reading books and studying, searching for that elusive "something extra" that, once acquired, will make them commanding individuals. In my experience, I've never met anyone who found that elusive "something extra" outside of themselves. Of course, good information, insights, and some well-chosen tools can certainly help but, as with creativity, I believe authentic confident living comes by shedding what's in the way of your power, not by adding something you think is missing.

Think about the times when you've been strongly influenced by another's words or actions. Were you moved with fancy techniques, polished moves and a slick delivery? Often, the most empowering situations happen when an individual drops all pretenses and just speaks from the heart – when everything else falls away and all that's left is the truth.

So what is the stuff that's in the way? What are the barriers we need to shed to let our power through? Here are some barriers I've noticed over the years, along with examples of the types of questions that pop into our heads while they're blocking our power.

Ego: How do I look? Do they like me?

Politics: How will this affect my career? How can I protect my turf?

Self-Doubt: Why am I here? I can't do this.

Self-Talk: You idiot! You always say the wrong thing!

Manipulation: How can I make them do what I want? I'll play on their emotions.

Masks: I can't let them see the real me.

Perfectionism: I must be perfect at all times – show no fear – make everyone happy.

If you want to be more creative, an artist will tell you to shake off what's getting in the way. So what would be left after you cast off these barriers? What would flow freely, given an unobstructed path? Imagine no fluff, no posturing, no gimmicks, and no mechanics – just the real, authentic, and most powerful *you*.

O-Blocks

"What did you love to do when you were a child? Because that's when you probably had a clearer idea of who you were, what you loved and what you wanted to be when you grew up."

– Pat Lynch, originator of the phrase,
"Thinking outside the box"

What's preventing you from living your dream? Over the years, I have met countless people living their dreams and at least as many others who didn't believe they could make their dreams happen – the challenges were just too great. Stacey Mayo, author of *I Can't Believe I Get Paid To Do This!*, has nicknamed these challenges "O-Blocks": obstacles that block us and appear so large that we can't see our way around them. For many people, the obstacles to living out their dreams seem larger than the dreams themselves. When you focus on the obstacles, they become all you see.

Let me give you a simple example. John and Mandy are driving separately to work and both encounter a sign reading, "Caution road construction ahead." John becomes angry and frustrated – he is running behind and this new hassle will make him late for an important meeting. Grumbling, John joins the long line of vehicles moving snail-like through the construction zone. Mandy, also running late, stops at the sign to weigh her options. After some consideration, she chooses an alternate route, bypasses the road construction and arrives at work in time for her meeting.

And so it goes for living your dreams. Focusing on obstacles such as fear of failure, lack of expertise or time will paralyze you. When you focus on your vision, you can easily brainstorm ways to get past obstacles in your course.

Here are some common O-Blocks that stop people. Which ones resonate with you?

Marital status or age

1. I am married and have to support my family.
2. I'm too old; maybe if I were younger.

Lack of expertise, credibility, belief in self

1. I don't know how to do it.
2. I'm not smart/talented enough.

Financial, time, scarcity

1. I'll do it when I'm more financially secure.
2. I can't make money doing it.
3. I'll lose my company health benefits.

4. There's not enough time.

Approval from others

1. What will people say/think of me?
2. My family won't understand/approve.

Fear of success

1. Others will be jealous of my success.
2. I'll have to move to a bigger/smaller center.
3. I'll lose my friends/connections.

Fear of failure or pain

1. I've tried before and failed.
2. What if this isn't it?
3. What if I fail?

Most of these statements are directly related to our fears. Many are scarcity-related dialogues. There's a truism I use in my workshops, "What is expected tends to be realized." If you believe your dreams are possible, then they are. The secret is to believe in your dreams and yourself, take action, and allow them to unfold.

Here are some tips to help you conquer fear and bring your dreams into reality. Visualize what it is you want to have happen. Imagine it has already appeared in your life. Script it out, write the story of your dream as if it has already happened and make it exciting and fantastic. Notice the questions you are asking yourself. Do they help you move forward or keep you stuck? Ask yourself, "What can I do today to make my dream a reality?"

Finally, change the "O" in "O-Blocks" to "opportunities" that challenge us and encourage us to look for creative ways to overcome obstacles and live our dreams.

Garden-Variety "Shoulds"

"Every waking moment, we talk to ourselves about the things we experience. Our self-talk, the thoughts we communicate to ourselves, in turn control the way we feel and act."

– John Lembo, author

Many of us live with a long list of "shoulds" – our beliefs or expectations as to how the world works and how others and we should conduct ourselves. Here are a few examples. Everyone should arrive at work on time. Businesses should treat me with respect. My colleagues should always support and cooperate with me. I should not make mistakes. I should be better at this. I should be able to handle any situation in my life. The list goes on.

Make a conscious decision to be aware of your "shoulditis." How often do you find yourself thinking or saying the word "should"? If you're like most people, this word is used often and endlessly. If the "shoulds" are directed at others, the frustration from unfulfilled expectations can be overwhelming. When directed toward ourselves, the guilt can be debilitating. Add up the number of negative "should" statements you give yourself daily and multiply it by 365 (days in the year). Then ask yourself, "Who is making me feel lacking? Who keeps inundating me with messages that produce guilt?"

Our should/ought/must talk is tied to expectations others have programmed into us. The lower our self-esteem, the more loudly this voice clamors for perfection. If our negative self-talk is forceful, our self-esteem gets swatted every time we fall short.

Now, I'm not talking about such shoulds as traffic laws or the moral shoulds of positive religious conviction. If you only use these, you're unlikely to damage your self-esteem. "I should not steal," or, "I must not cheat on my income tax," are not the shoulds that do us in. The common, garden-variety shoulds beat us down daily.

Certain of society's shoulds are basic rules made to protect the rights of all. Some shoulds go to make up what we call a healthy conscience. People with healthy self-esteem understand the difference between negative and positive shoulds. If they transgress, they don't beat themselves up with endless guilt. Rather, they own up to the offence, apologize, and make amends. They accept the responsibility for their behavior.

You can send yourself the same general message without battering your self-worth. Instead of should, switch to words like "want to," "choose," "prefer," "wish" or "desire."

Notice the difference here.

(Judgmental/Critical)
I should have done a better job.
(Non-judgmental/-self-responsible)
I wish I'd chosen to do the job better. (Implied: I own up to the fact that I am responsible for the caliber of my work.)
(Judgmental/Critical)
I should go or I'll be late for work.
(Non-judgmental/-self-responsible)
I want to go, as I don't choose to be late for work. (Implied: I do not want to pay for the consequences of tardiness.)

In each case, the initial judgmental/critical statement reinforces feelings of guilt. The revised self-talk is a clear-cut reinforcement that you have a choice and that you are responsible for your choices. Notice that self-punishment, self-lecturing, and self-blame are absent in the non-judgmental/self-responsible statements.

Remember, negative self-talk (shoulditis) is laced with control, blame, and manipulation. Positive self-talk is based on faith, inner choice, and the acceptance of personal responsibility. Positive self-talk takes the form of intent, of commitment, of being in charge of your own destiny. Positive self-talk continually reminds you that you are the chooser.

Which kind of talk do you specialize in? Start listening.

What If?

"Fear is that little darkroom where negatives are developed."

– Michael Pritchard, keynote speaker and facilitator

The water was getting deeper and I thought, "What if I die?"

It was 1965. So much snow had fallen that winter that drifts covered the tops of the highest fence posts. My mother has a picture of my brother and I sitting on a snowdrift as high as our porch roof. When spring finally arrived, the melting snow filled rivers, creeks, and dugouts to overflowing – whole sections of roadways washed away.

A neighboring family came to help us move cattle that spring. As water had already crossed the road near the meadow, father met them at the intersection of the main road with a tractor and grain wagon. All piled in the wagon for a slow ride to the farm.

By late afternoon the road was impassible, even by tractor, drowned beneath a foot or more of fast flowing water. Father had to take the neighbors back to their vehicle, so he decided to strike off across country with tractor and wagon, through the fields, to the main road. I was allowed to ride along this time.

The tractor and wagon lurched along the trail leading to the east pasture. Before long, we were heading across country – water cascading off the big back tractor tires.

The excitement and anxiety of the trip reminded me of a carnival ride and kept my heart skipping beats and my eyes wide open. As the water grew deeper, I began to count all the possible ways I could die. My mind was filled with "what ifs."

At one point, the back wheel of the tractor dropped into a hole, throwing father up against the fender. The wagon pitched and shuddered, tossing us violently back and forth.

Eventually, we left the water behind and were soon rolling down the gravel road en route to the intersection. The ride home was less stressful – free of "what ifs."

The "what if" game can immobilize us – freeze us with its frightening possibilities. Have you ever noticed that the "what if" game is like an elevator that always takes you to the bottom floor – the lowest place that we could possibly go? The elevator doesn't stop at the middle floors, giving us a chance to consider alternatives.

Fears and doubts settle in and, before we know it, we're procrastinating – or worse yet finding ourselves in a state of paralysis where we can't seem to do anything at all.

As long as I can remember, a ceramic plaque has hung in my mother's kitchen. Written on it is the Serenity Prayer: God grant me the serenity to accept the things I cannot change, courage to change the things I can, and wisdom to know the difference.

New York Yankees outfielder Mickey Rivers put it this way: "There ain't no sense worrying about things you got no control over."

When you stop worrying, when you stop playing the "what if" game, you begin to see situations clearly and can choose an effective, well considered strategy. The truth is, most of the "what if" scenarios I have imagined over the years simply never happened. My anxieties and worries proved unfounded. I have forgotten most of the fears that once kept me awake at night.

As with that ride in the wagon so many years ago, letting go of the "what ifs" made the experience enjoyable. I suspect the same can be said about that "what if" that worries you.

Assumptions

"The harder you fight to hold on to specific assumptions, the more likely there's gold in letting go of them."

– John Seely Brown, chief scientist of Xerox

I love what Don Miguel Ruiz has to say about assumptions in his inspiring best-seller, *The Four Agreements*. In fact, Ruiz's Agreement Number 3 is "Don't make assumptions."

Ruiz says, "Find the courage to ask questions and to express what you really want. Communicate with others as clearly as you can to avoid misunderstandings, sadness and drama. With just this one agreement, you can completely transform your life."

Here's one true (and dramatic) account I read recently in Iris Benrudy's fine newsletter *Simply Success* – available at simplysuccess.ca. The story is drawn from the police log of Sarasota, Fla. It is a frightening, yet humorous example of high drama resulting from an assumption that takes place in a grocery store parking lot.

An elderly lady was coming from the grocery store to her car and saw four males in the act of leaving her vehicle. She dropped her shopping bags and drew her handgun, shouting, "I have a gun and I know how to use it. Get out of the car!"

The four men took off and ran like mad. The lady, shaken, loaded her shopping bags into the car and got into the driver's seat. She was so shaken that she could not get her key into the ignition. She tried and tried, then noticed that there was a football, a Frisbee and two cases of beer in the front seat.

Shocked, she looked around and saw her own car parked a few spaces farther down. She loaded her bags into the car and drove to the police station to report her mistake. The sergeant to whom she told the story couldn't stop laughing. He pointed to the other end of the counter where four pale young men were reporting a carjacking by a crazy elderly woman. No charges were filed.

The moral of this twisted tale is: check your assumptions! Better yet, don't make assumptions!

Daily, we do make assumptions about things, situations, or people and often without the benefit of full awareness. Our assumptions stem from two main hypotheses.

A) We assume what *seems* obvious; no explanation is necessary.

B) We assume what is not so obvious; an explanation is required. Therefore, we create one.

In Byron Katie's bestseller, *Loving What Is*, Katie calls assumptions uninvestigated thoughts. Katie introduces us to what she calls "inquiry." She suggests we continually ask, "Is this true? Do I absolutely know that what I'm assuming is true?"

Assumption: Bob didn't call last night. He must be upset with me. Inquiry: Is it true Bob didn't call because he's upset? Can I absolutely know that Bob is upset?

If you're brave and wish to take the process of inquiry a step further, ask yourself, "Does this thought bring me peace or stress?" and, "Who would I be, in the presence of this person (or persons), without this thought?" Inquiry challenges you to seek the truth. Try it – the insights can be quite astounding.

Never assume that things are the way they appear on the surface. Always check out the facts and never rush to a conclusion. Says Ruiz, "What we think we understand about what someone says, how someone looks at us, what someone means by what they do or say may often not reflect reality at all, and more often than not lead us to think badly of ourselves or of others, and reinforce not being *impeccable with our word*." (This, by the way, is his Agreement Number 1.)

Take Your Foot Off the Brake

"It isn't the actual truth about yourself and your abilities that hurts you – it's the things that you consider true and that have no basis in truth."

– Brian Tracy, speaker, motivator, business trainer

Our subconscious mind has no sense of humor, plays no jokes, and cannot discern the difference between reality and an imagined thought or image. What we continually hold in our mind will eventually manifest in our lives. Unfortunately, most of us are completely unaware of this fact and so do not monitor our thoughts with the thoroughness needed to create the lives we want. And since most of us simply don't feel worthy or deserving of prosperity, radiant health, or success, these unmonitored thoughts override our good intentions and sabotage our best efforts.

The fact is, you do deserve every good thing that you are capable of acquiring as the result of your many talents. You need to develop your self-beliefs to the point where they serve you every day in a positive way. Men and women who accomplish extraordinary things are just ordinary people who have overcome the obstacles that stood in their way.

In her exceptional book *You Can Heal Your Life*, Louise Hay claims everyone has feelings of inferiority occasionally. We may think we're not as good as other people or good enough to acquire and enjoy the things that we want in life. Even if we work hard and achieve some worthwhile objectives, we may still believe we are not entitled to our successes. This may prompt us to engage in behaviors that sabotage our successes.

The most harmful beliefs are the ones we refer to as "self-limiting." These are beliefs about yourself, most of which are untrue, that put the brakes on your success.

The starting point for personal change comes when you work up the courage to question each belief seriously. Check your facts. Challenge your assumptions. Ask yourself, "What presumptions am I making about myself or a situation that might not be true?" The fact is, we often wear our excuses and negative assumptions like a comfortable old pair of shoes. We fall in love with our reasons for not moving ahead.

Richard Bach, author of *Illusions*, wrote, "Argue for your limitations, and sure enough, they're yours." Often, we become the prosecuting attorney in the case against ourselves. We dispute, argue, and attempt to prove to ourselves and others that our limitations are real. In addition, the less justification these ideas or beliefs have, the more adamant we become in attempting to prove them to others. Whatever they are, resolve to challenge them. Hold each belief up to the light and see it for what it really is: reality or illusion?

Here are three steps you can take immediately to put these ideas into action. First, accept that you are as good and as talented in your own way as anyone else you will ever meet. If you really want it, you can accomplish anything! Second, challenge a belief or idea about yourself that is holding you back. What if you had extraordinary ability in that area? What difference would that make in your life? Third, stop making excuses for lack of success. Instead, start making progress. Think and talk about what you want and then get busy making it come true.

We all have ideas or attitudes about ourselves and our abilities that hold us back from enjoying success and happiness. The good news is we can rid ourselves of the false ideas that block our full potential.

The Dream, Big and Beautiful, Comes First.

"Don't be afraid of the space between your dreams and reality. If you can dream, you can make it so."

– Belva Davis, award winning broadcast journalist

It was Career Day at the high school and the counselor was making his rounds, chatting with students. He stopped to ask my daughter what career she had chosen to pursue. "I dream of making a million dollars as a writer," she replied. "Just like my dad."

The counselor was impressed. "Your dad made a million dollars as a writer?"

"No," my daughter replied. "But he sure dreams about it a lot."

The dream, big and beautiful, comes first. Then the effort to realize it begins.

"There are only two kinds of people in this world," said humorist, Robert Orben, "the realists and the dreamers. The realists know where they're going. The dreamers have already been there." I love this quotation because it affirms the value of dreaming. I think most successful people strike a balance between dreaming big and setting realistic goals. So what stands in the way of dreaming big in your own life?

The following are three of the most significant barriers. As you review each, ask yourself whether one or more of these roadblocks are keeping you from really going after what you want from life.

Fear

Vincent van Gogh said, "The fishermen know that the sea is dangerous and the storm terrible, but they have never found these dangers sufficient reason for remaining ashore." Is there a particular fear that is keeping you from venturing out on the big sea of possibility? Fear of failure? Loss of security? Fear of criticism or judgment? Before you pack up ship, ask yourself what's the worst that could happen by striving to reach your dream. If the best that could happen outweighs the worst, move forward with confidence.

Lack of knowledge

Just because you don't know all the details, that's no reason to keep from dreaming big. History is strewn with great discoveries that came because a daring soul ventured into the unknown with a big dream. If lack of knowledge is your excuse for not pursuing your dreams, ask yourself, "What is the least I need to know in order to go for it?" or, "Where do I go, whom do I see, to acquire the necessary skills?"

Negative associations

"Keep away from people who try to belittle your ambitions," said Mark Twain. "Small people always do that, but the really great make you feel that you too can become great." With what type of people do you associate? Are they people who become as excited as you when sharing your goals, desires, and dreams? Will they hold you accountable for doing the things you need and challenge you to keep on going? "Show me whom you frequent," reads a French proverb, "and I will tell you who you are."

Greg Anderson, best-selling author and founder of the American Wellness Project puts it this way: "When we are motivated by goals that have deep meaning, by dreams that need completion, by pure love that needs expressing, then we truly live."

Perhaps your dreams *will* bring you a million dollars – or simply the satisfaction that comes with setting worthwhile goals and then achieving them. The truth is any worthy goal must first be dreamed before it can be accomplished. Pursue your passion and have the courage to dream big and know that if you can dream big, you can make it so.

A New Way to Think

"Most folks are about as happy as they make up their minds to be."

– Abraham Lincoln

Recently, while facilitating a workshop on self-esteem, a participant approached me with a question. "Why am I a sponge for negativity?" I asked her for clarification. "No matter how hard I try to be positive, I always end up focusing on the negative." She went on to explain that her intention is to be positive. Yet, despite her best efforts, her constant focus is on the negative, keeping her frustrated and depressed.

There simply wasn't enough time between breaks at the workshop to delve into the issue. I'd like to take some time now to answer the question. It's important to understand that she may have been thinking in a negative way for some time now. Negative thoughts can be difficult to spot because they become a habit – they flash quickly into your mind. Most of us are not used to "watching" our thoughts – we're simply reacting to them. Learning to spot and catch these negative thoughts is a skill anyone can master with time. When you are depressed, your thoughts are distorted in a negative way. These are called "thinking errors." Here are some common examples. Spot the ones that apply to you.

Over generalizing: thinking everything is going wrong when only one thing has gone awry. You make one mistake and think, "I can't do anything right!"

Arguing away the positive: "He says he likes me, but he just feels sorry for me."

Making negative predictions: "I can't do that; it'll be a disaster."

Taking things personally or taking the blame for what others do: "My son failed his math exam. I should have helped him more. I am a bad parent," or "My partner has left me. I'm not deserving of a happy relationship."

Exaggerating the negative: "This is a complete disaster, a total failure."

It may take a lot of practice to change these ways. Be aware, your initial efforts may trigger more negative thoughts such as, "It's not working. I can't do anything right." Give yourself time to learn and grow. Here are some suggestions to get started.

First, write down your negative thoughts as soon as possible. If it's difficult to notice a specific thought, try noticing when you feel negative and ask, "What went through my mind just before I started feeling negative?" Watch for your negativity triggers.

Second, ask yourself, "Is what I believe *true*?" It may be useful to consult someone outside the situation for an unbiased opinion. Would everyone have the same belief in this situation? Examine other possible explanations for the event occurring. Try a real-life experiment. For example, if your friend doesn't phone, call him or her to ask why. Challenge your assumption that he didn't call because he was upset with you.

Third, remember that you are in total control of how you choose to perceive life. Choose to fill your world (and organization) with opportunity and unbridled enthusiasm.

We all have the power to change. It is only a matter of examining our attitudes and desires. Then we can make a conscientious choice to help ourselves. As long as we are aware of our own attitudes and are willing to change what we don't like, change can and will occur. Perception dictates the way you see the world. Remember: you are in control of your own reality.

Accommodate/Assimilate/Discard

"Do we really see each other for what we really are, or do we just see what we want to see, the image distorted by our own personal lenses? I lost someone today and the funny thing is, I don't even know who she was."

– Jeff Melvoin, actor, *Northern Exposure, Lovers and Madmen*

Sometimes, when working in the field of self-esteem and personal development, we become so focused on helping others to learn, grow, and reach their full potential that we don't stop to consider how much we have grown – not just as coaches and facilitators, but as human beings. Then someone comes along and provides us with a "snapshot" of our own personal growth and development. That revelation can be quite startling. Recently, I had an encounter that opened my eyes to how we "pigeon-hole" the people in our lives – assuming they are who they are and they will never change.

Here's what happened when I met an acquaintance I hadn't seen for some time.

"Hey, (Acquaintance) – it's been a long time. How are you doing?"

"Surviving – getting by. How about you?"

"It's going great. I'm having such fun helping people grow their self-esteem."

"Grow their what?"

"Their self-esteem – how they feel about themselves – helping them discover their gifts and live a happy life."

(Confused.) "OK. Just how are you doing that?"

"Have you seen my column in the *Red Deer Advocate?"*

"I don't read the paper." (Apologies to my editor.)

"I'm also doing workshops and I'm speaking to groups and businesses. It's an exciting time. Every time I turn around, there's another opportunity to learn and share."

"You're speaking to groups?"

"All the time – it's a lot of fun and I love the chance to share my ideas."

"I can't see you speaking to groups. You're way too quiet and reserved."

(Pondering the statement.) "Things change."

"Yeah, but people don't."

Admittedly, there was a time when I was quiet and reserved – all the time. I still prefer, at times, to sit back quietly and listen rather than be center of attention. The difference is, I now make a conscious choice to do so and I'm no longer motivated by fear of being ridiculed or challenged. I've worked long and hard to move beyond my original programming and self-defeating beliefs. People *do* change and you can, too!

So, what happens when someone refuses to fit into the pigeonhole? We accommodate, assimilate, or discard. Let's say we decide an individual is a certain way for whatever the reason. We put our stamp on that person with labels like aggressive, reserved, honest, dishonest – whatever.

Should an individual act, speak, or behave in a manner contradictory to our stamp, we have a problem. The reserved person is now acting assertive or the aggressive person is being quiet and reflective. We have a choice to make. We can *accommodate* the new behavior and allow for the fact that quiet people are occasionally aggressive, or aggressive people can sometimes be quiet and reflective. We may choose to *assimilate* this new information and revise our estimation of the individual. We may think or say such things as, "Perhaps I've misjudged Bob. I thought he was 'hardheaded' but I see now that he can be quite open to new ideas." We can also (as with my acquaintance above) *discard* the contradictory information entirely.

I'm not suggesting that everyone deserves multiple chances to redeem him or herself. Use your good judgment. In my experience, some people simply *choose* not to make positive change and your initial assessment may be totally accurate. Just remember, situations do change, people can change, and so should your perceptions.

What's on Your Mind?

"And so we fail, even though we're doing our best, not because we can't win ... but because we're trying to use a bunch of tired old options, choices, and strategies that aren't working anymore."

– Pat Lynch, author of *The Five Secrets You're Not Supposed to Know*

Years ago, when I was practicing therapeutic hypnosis, I helped people stop smoking. Repeatedly, a smoker would tell me he or she felt controlled by cigarettes. I would remind the smoker that there still was a choice to make: to smoke or not to smoke.

"But why do I have such a strong desire to smoke?"

"The decision to smoke seemed appropriate at the time of that first puff," I would often explain. "The subconscious mind is still operating on that initial decision."

Sometimes, our choices take on a life of their own. They operate under our mental radar. It's not unlike "spyware" programs, which operate covertly in the background of computers, robbing memory, corrupting files, using up valuable resources. And, as with the computer, old choices impact our ability to function and to process information effectively. If life were simple, we would merely install a human "anti-spyware" program, press scan, and reveal the number of unconscious mental processes at work under the surface.

"Look, Bob. You have 57 self-defeating beliefs running in the background of your personality: lack of deservability, feelings of inferiority, fear of responsibility…."

We make decisions based on the best informat
As children, we try to fit into a mysterious worlc
to survive there. We take on the attitudes of thos

erful and all knowing, such as parents, teachers, and spiritual leaders, all in an attempt to gain acceptance, safety, and security. Then we grow up, our life situations change and we no longer need the old survival strategies. Yet we continue to be influenced by earlier programming and seldom do we re-examine our old attitudes and ideas.

Background programs can be physical, such as smoking or overeating to avoid uncomfortable feelings or to deal with stress. They can be mental/emotional programs, such as feeling like a victim, having low self-esteem, difficulties with money, or negative thinking. Past choices were reasonable at a specific time and place in our lives, but now may actually be hurting us. And unless we give the subconscious different instructions, it will continue to activate those old programs, thinking it's still what you want. The subconscious mind was designed to be our servant, yet many of us let it run the show.

The first step in rearranging the mental landscape is awareness; in this case, becoming aware of when habitual programming (an old belief system) is activated. Our smoker might assume he or she smokes all the time, but might be amazed to discover that certain times, places, and situations trigger the desire to puff. The same is true of people with self-esteem issues. They may feel competent doing their job, but as soon as someone criticizes them, they feel inept. Once we recognize when the mental program begins to run, we can work on retraining the subconscious.

The next time you feel an old pattern begin to assert itself, whether it's smoking or any number of undesirable habits, stop, step back from your initial reaction, and look for the trigger. Am I stressed? Has someone made an unkind comment? Has someing I've witnessed brought back a childhood memory? The subconscious must follow the directions of the conscious mind. When you make a new choice, and act on it every time, the inner mind will eventually follow – all subsequent action will be based on the new decision.

Check Your Self-Talk

"The first order of business of anyone who wants to enjoy success in all areas of his her life is to take charge of the internal dialogue they have and only think, say and behave in a manner consistent with the results they truly desire."

– Sidney Madwed, writer, speaker, motivator

Have you ever made a disparaging comment about yourself and had someone say to you, "Check your self-talk"? Self-talk is the constant stream of chatter that goes on in your head (and mine, and the head of everyone else, for that matter).

Take some time to notice what you say to yourself and how you say it. Do you constantly criticize yourself, how people treat you, your faults, or the injustices of life? Imagine that you had an 'invisible friend' that went around with you all day, every day, and was constantly whispering comments like these in your ear! How would you feel at the end of a day? At the end of a week? After a month of such programming?

Well, guess what! You're already doing this to yourself and in a far more effective manner than an invisible friend could ever do it. After all, if friends treated you like that they wouldn't remain your friends for long. And because you're doing it to yourself, and probably have since childhood, you may no longer notice it or recognize the powerful impact your internal dialogue has on your mood and attitude towards yourself and life.

For example, you might compare yourself to people at work or in the community and tell yourself that you'll never be as successful or popular as they will. This may lead you to believe you're not good enough to talk to these people or to feelings of insecurity when around them. Your insecurity may even lead you to feel bitterness or anger toward certain individuals and that is certainly counter-productive for all parties concerned.

Think about the people you know. Doesn't it seem like the people who expect to succeed in life and business tend to do so? There's an old adage: "What is expected tends to be realized." Even doctors agree that patients typically heal as quickly or as slowly as they expect to. Here's another truism: "As you imagine, so shall it become true."

Consider this: if another person said nasty things about you each time he saw you, not only would you dislike that person greatly, you might try to avoid him at all cost. You can't avoid yourself, so you need to treat yourself the way you would a best friend. A best friend would always be supportive and speak to you in a positive way. As a result, he would make you feel good about yourself and you would want to spend more time with him. And seeing that you're going to be spending every minute of every hour of every day with yourself, it makes sense to be nice to yourself.

Our negative self-talk is pernicious and demoralizing and debilitating. And because we are so used to it, we don't consciously pay attention to it and therefore do not challenge it. It goes on and on in the background and the effect is that we are giving ourselves powerful subconscious suggestions to feel bad!

Each time you recognise that you are doing your self-criticizing or self-undermining, pause, remind yourself that it's just an old habit and, from now on, you're changing this habit. Positive self-talk helps you calm yourself down, feel more confident, and see things in perspective but, most importantly, it helps to build a positive, supportive relationship with yourself. This is important to have so you can build good relationships with others and get what you want out of life. Remember, positive minds attract positive people and experiences.

Seeking Clarity

"Extremists think 'communication' means agreeing with them."
– Leo Rosten, American teacher, academic and humorist

Occasionally, the topic of clarifying expectations comes up at the office or during one of my workshops. Essentially, clarifying expectations means both parties involved in an interaction are completely clear about what they're asking for, what they expect, and when they expect to get it.

The topic invariably sends me back to my childhood. Many years ago, a salesperson showed up at the door of our farmhouse selling air compressors. After explaining why his product was superior to all other models, he began talking about the many accessories available – among them, a professional quality paint sprayer (ideal for painting corrals and granaries). Referring to a note pad, he listed off the names of neighbors who had already taken advantage of this time-limited offer.

Father asked him to bring the compressor to our shop and give us a demonstration. It easily inflated tires, blew the dust from old air filters and, thanks to an impressive assortment of useful accessories, would certainly improve the efficiency of our farming operation. Impressed with the product and sales pitch, Father wrote a check and shook the man's hand. We could expect delivery within a week to 10 days.

Some time later, the salesperson returned – his truck box filled with cardboard boxes. Once hauled out from the box, our new compressor seemed, somehow, smaller than the model we had seen demonstrated earlier. We were told it wasn't. It came with a length of hose and a couple of attachments, but that was it. Evidently, useful accessories (like the paint sprayer) were expensive options not included in the base price. For an extra $60, we could come away with all the available accessories in a handy tote case.

Father complained bitterly to the salesperson, who denied ever saying the accessories were included in the base price. The conversation quickly degenerated to the point where Father threatened to shove the air compressor where the sun didn't shine. Aggravated, the sales person picked up a box containing the accessories (minus the handy tote) and tossed it at Father. He suggested Father shove it in an equally dark locale, climbed into his truck, and roared out of the yard, boxes tumbling around in the back of his truck box.

Who was at fault? I don't know, but I do know that conflict arises when expectations are unclear. An angry outburst could have been avoided had both parties remained calm after the miscommunication was exposed. Developing your self-esteem will help you to ask the right questions, and to stand up for what you believe to be right, rather than letting people manipulate you and then exploding or backing off for fear the mistake is yours.

Some expectations in relationships are implicit, like your boss expecting you to be at work on time. Yet, many expectations need to be explicit, requiring further clarification. Negative situations are created when you assume your expectations are self-evident and clearly understood by others. In new relationships or business dealings, get all the expectation out on the table at the beginning. Clearly articulate who does or gets what. Almost all relationship difficulties are a result of ambiguous expectations around roles and goals.

It's easy to pretend differences don't exist and to hope things will work out. Investing time and effort up front to clarify expectations will save time and effort in the future. Seeking clarity allows us to turn stumbling blocks into building blocks. Hence, be clear about what you're asking for, what you expect, and when you expect to get it. Any questions?

Boundaries

"We teach people how to treat us."

– Phillip C. (Dr. Phil) McGraw

It was just after noon when I pulled into the gas station across the street from where I worked. The year was 1981 and I was still driving a gas-guzzling chunk of mid-'70s Mopar muscle.

The "Ding!" of the station bell alerted the attendant of my arrival. An older man trudged around the side of my car and stared down at me.

I held up a $10 bill. (Enough to buy half a tank of gas!)

"Ten dollars, please," I said and the man grunted. I watched him fumbling with the nozzle, and then heard the familiar clatter of the old gas pump.

I looked down at the bills I planned to pay over lunch hour. When I glanced up, I saw the dial on the pump pass $17.

"Stop!" I yelled out the window. "That's too much!"

The attendant returned to my window and glared at me.

"I said $10," I said, waving the bill.

"You said fill 'er up," snapped the attendant.

"No," I insisted. "I said $10."

"Well, you *got* $17.53," stated the attendant, pointing to the pump.

Angry now, I snapped back, "Well all I *got* is 10 bucks!"

He stared at me hard for a few seconds and then snatched the bill from my hand. I heard him cursing something about young punks as he stomped back into the station.

Dr. Phil McGraw says, "We teach people how to treat us." Either we teach people to treat us with dignity and respect or we don't.

This means we are partly responsible for the mistreatment that we get at the hands of someone else. We shape others' behavior when we teach them what they can get away with and what they cannot.

The best way to "teach" someone how to treat us is to establish healthy boundaries. People need to know when they are acting in a way that is acceptable to us. Boundaries define limits. Boundaries can be flexible, expandable, and even impenetrable depending upon the situation.

You know you need to set a boundary if you find yourself dealing with constant anger, complaining, disregard, or inappropriate comments. When you set a limit or boundary with someone, do it clearly, preferably without anger and in as few words as possible.

It is important to state aloud what action upset you and to precede the emotion elicited with "I feel." By saying, "When you speak to me in that tone of voice (action), I feel hurt (emotion)," you are taking ownership of the feeling.

When you say only "I *am* angry or I *am* hurt," you are stating that the feeling is who you are. Emotions do not define us; they are a form of internal communication that helps us to understand ourselves.

Keep in mind, the worst thing you could do is make a lot of noise about establishing new boundaries, only to revert to the old, familiar patterns. To talk about boundaries and then not stand firm will teach others to regard our statements and declarations lightly.

Before expecting others to treat you with dignity, first treat yourself with dignity and respect. Never give anyone the opportunity to mistreat you. If you're not being treated the way you desire, then find out why! Be honest and forthright with yourself and others.

The Lady in the Green Car

"How we do one thing is how we do everything."

– Buddha

Every morning I used to take a similar route to work and, with rare exception, I had an encounter with The Lady in the Green Car. I don't know if she was consistently late getting out the door in the morning or just an aggressive driver. Whatever the reason, she became a source of frustration and a test of my patience each morning. It was not unusual to witness her making illegal lane changes, speeding, swerving through traffic, or tailgating.

One morning, I saw that she was driving a snappy new import model. She must have traded in her older North American model coupe. No doubt, the new model had better acceleration and responsiveness – crucial when darting in and out of traffic or accelerating rapidly through amber lights. Perhaps, this young woman was a frustrated stunt driver.

Buddha said, "How we do one thing is how we do everything." Accepting this statement as true, I'm left wondering how the "lady" moves through her personal and professional life. Does she rush through her days, never stopping to reflect or consider consequences? Is she impulsive? Does she make snap judgments then abruptly change her mind and direction? Does she comment without a thought toward appropriateness?

I believe the above statement by the great Buddha expresses a profound truth. Let's say I have a deep-seated belief that life is a competition pitting me against everyone else on the planet. Abundance is limited and I need to step on people to get to the front of the line. So stated, my tactic for dealing with life might be to rush headlong through it, bowling over anyone in my way. This plan of attack would be evident in everything I did, from driving to work and shopping to interacting with colleagues, friends and family.

Now, let's imagine my philosophy for living is one of patience, tolerance, and confident expectation. I believe that everyone has something of value to share with me and that people really are good at heart. My approach might be to seek the lesson from every experience, to treat people with respect, and to expect good things to arrive in my life.

It's easy to see how beliefs ripple through our lives and those of people around us. If you glimpse a non-productive theme playing itself out in one or more areas of your life, how should you go about changing your attitude? Certainly, the thought of changing your approach, attitudes, and beliefs on a grand scale seems tremendously overwhelming.

Let's return to the wisdom of Buddha for a moment and see what happens if we alter the statement slightly by adding the word "change" into the equation.

"Change how you do one thing, change how you do everything." When I changed my approach in one area of my life – being more patient with my children, for example – I began to notice changes in other areas. Positive change in one area has a positive ripple effect in your life and in the lives of those around you. And each change makes the next one easier. Try it!

As for the Lady in the Green Car, perhaps she is a cheerful, well-balanced individual who just happens to be an atrocious driver. All the same, I think I'll leave a little earlier for work and avoid the frustration.

Loser/User

"People who have no weaknesses are terrible. There is no way of taking advantage of them."

– Anatole France, French novelist

A colleague of mine recently described her girlfriend's partner as a loser/user. I asked her to expound upon the term. "You know the type," she said. "He's taking her for all she's worth." She went on explain how this individual was taking advantage of her friend's kind and generous nature: running up her credit cards, using and abusing her vehicle, contributing nothing financially to the household.

I thought about her comments for a moment. The world is filled with emotional predators – loser/users, if you like – and this individual certainly appeared to fall into that category. The question I posed to my colleague was, "Does your girlfriend understand why this is happening?"

Emotional predators control, use, and psychologically abuse friends, relatives, and even total strangers. By manipulating situations and people for their own purposes, these emotional leeches gain an upper hand and a sense of control. Many of these predators know exactly how much frustration, anger, and anxiety they inflict. Others carry on virtually oblivious of the harm they cause, and victims are many times unaware of the damage being inflicted upon their self-esteem.

Why might you fall victim to an emotional predator? Do you have a vague notion that everyone else is somehow more important than you are (your partner, parents, friends, or family)? It's well worth asking yourself why. Some people would have you believe you have only two choices in life: either you focus only on yourself and don't give a damn whom you manipulate, control, or hurt (I don't care who I step on to get to the top!) or you focus only on others and let them use, abuse, and manipulate you (I don't deserve anything better!). Both options are equally flawed and mutually destructive.

Many decent people mistakenly choose the "I don't deserve" route. They say to themselves, "I don't want anything for myself. I just want to make everyone else happy." Does this sound familiar? Have you tried to follow and justify this approach, putting yourself into a subordinate position? What people or situations have you attracted into your life?

If you feel trapped, imprisoned, if you allow others to take advantage of you, if you are always trying to please others, if you find yourself frequently over-explaining yourself or apologizing when it is unnecessary, then you need to open up those psychological prison doors.

The notion that others are more important than you are destroys your life and happiness – especially when it becomes your approach to life. It typically targets your self-esteem and limits your ability to discover your own interests and values in life. Acknowledging your skills and valuing your uniqueness is essential to your happiness.

I am not excusing the appalling behavior of the emotional predator, nor am I placing the responsibility for resolving a difficult situation solely upon the shoulders of the injured party. I am suggesting a healthier alternative to the bully or slave version of life. To reach your full growth and to enjoy your life to its fullest, it is essential that you take an active interest in yourself. You cannot let others determine the course of your life and expect peace of mind. Standing up for you is one of the most challenging yet powerful human acts that can eliminate guilt, overcome fear, and make anger unnecessary.

Are You an Enabler?

"It's a false sense of caring if you always step in to fix things up for another person."

– Unknown

At a recent management seminar, the facilitator talked in detail about managing difficult behavior. She made a crucial statement: silence condones. Essentially, when we fail to address inappropriate behavior, we condone it. As managers, we had to ask ourselves, "Has our silence enabled staff members to proceed or progress in unproductive/inappropriate patterns of behavior?"

The statement stayed with me on the drive home along with a new term: enabling. This baffling phenomenon takes many forms, all with the same effect: allowing individuals to avoid the consequences of their actions.

A fine line exists between helping and enabling. Helping is doing something for people who are incapable of doing for themselves – from lack of time, talent, or experience. Enabling is doing something that they can and should be doing for themselves. We often begin enabling in an attempt to be kind and helpful.

Enabling occurs in a variety of situations and with everyone from life partners, co-workers, and children (adult or minor), to parents, friends, and siblings. The person(s) whose unhealthy patterns we enable may be exhibiting one or more of the following behaviors: drinking too much, overspending, gambling, working too much or not at all, maxing out the credit cards, abusing prescription or street drugs, getting arrested (with you bailing them out) or any number of other unhealthy behaviors/patterns of addiction.

As enabling behaviors become routine, we end up feeling frustrated, ineffectual, and angry. Often, we continue to enable because we don't want to appear mean or unreasonable. Enabling behaviors directly and indirectly supports the vicious cycle of never-ending problems and pain of addiction – whatever form that addiction should take. When we stop enabling, when we stop helping and covering up for addicts, we allow them to experience the consequences of their out-of-control behavior. We no longer wake them up, loan them money, or bail them out of jail. We stop shielding them from the consequences of their behaviors.

Sometimes enabling takes the form of a parent who is in denial about a child's misbehavior at school, on the playground, or in the neighborhood. Rather than acknowledging that there is a problem, the parent gets into a fight-and-defend mode, refusing to take responsibility for correcting the situation in a healthy way. Other examples include calling in to the boss to say a spouse is sick when he or she is actually hung over, or making excuses as to why your child didn't attend school, when he simply refused to get up in the morning. Enabling can be as simple as finishing up or doing the work of a co-worker who isn't pulling his or her share of the load. For many people, enabling is second nature.

So, how can we stop enabling? Start by setting boundaries and not making hollow threats. Carefully explain to the individual that boundaries have been set, and explain that these boundaries are for *you*, not for the other person. Once those boundaries have been established, stick to them! Do not take on responsibilities or duties that rightfully belong to another. Stop making excuses for someone else's behavior. It may even require removing yourself from a destructive situation or individual.

Why do we enable? There are many contributing factors, but one of the underlying reasons appears to be our own low self-esteem. We haven't cultivated the ability to say no without fear of losing the love or caring of that other person. Sometimes we say or do nothing out of fear: fear of reprisal, fear of the other person hating/hurting/not liking us, or fear of butting in where we don't think we belong.

Resisting the urge to enable becomes easier when you recognize it's happening, and take steps to build your own sense of self-worth. As you become stronger, healthier, whole, and learn to love yourself, you'll become more assertive in saying what you know to be true and constructive for you and those you love.

Busy Being Busy

"Being anxious, always in a rush and racing after whatever it is we've imagined will help us to be more at peace with ourselves, is like running to catch the shadow of a passing cloud on a hot summer's day so that we get to stand in a cool spot!"

– Guy Finley, writer, speaker, founder of the
Life of Learning Foundation

"I'm too busy to exercise. I never have enough time for family and friends. How can I read a book, listen to music, or relax when I've got so much to do?" Does this sound familiar? It seems we're all busy being busy. Where does the time go? Every day we awaken with a full day ahead of us and plenty of time to make a positive difference in our lives. However, at day's end, we're often left feeling we haven't made one bit of difference.

Attitude can play a big part. If you have the mind-set, "I'm just trying to get through the day," that's exactly what you'll do – just get through the day. When you adopt the attitude of, "Let's see how much I can accomplish today," you'll get a lot more done.

The truth is rushing through our lives does not produce more time, nor does it increase our productivity. To the contrary, rushing headlong through life limits our possibilities for discovering new and better ways to grow and enjoy this wonderful life. There isn't one of us who wouldn't like to get more done. Highly productive people do more and stress less. The question is how? Conventional wisdom leaves us with grim choices at best. Less sleep. More work. No fun.

The more productive we are inwardly, the greater our outer productivity. To get started, look at how you spend your time and why you're doing the things you do. In the same manner that certain foods fill our bellies but offer little nourishment, certain tasks can fill our days but return few benefits. Learn to say no to activities that just keep you busy but don't help you to accomplish anything.

Peace and productivity seem to oppose each other in the busy exterior world. With a watchful eye and re-evaluation of our busyness, the two can merge into an unstoppable energetic force. As anger, stress, anxiety, fear, and worry dwell less in our hearts, clarity, stillness, and a sharp mind become our new and constant companions.

We need to be at our personal best to give our personal best for our family, friends, and work associates. If we're at work and feeling guilty about yelling at the kids, not having dinner ready, or resentful that we had to miss a golf game to work on a weekend project, what frame of mind will we be in to greet our customers? Conversely, if our mind is filled with the demands of work, unfulfilled expectations or customer service issues, what frame of mind will we be in to greet and share time with loved ones?

Moreover, what does "busy" really mean? While we are redefining things, let's redefine "busy." Being busy can be a way of pushing aside something in our life we'd rather not deal with. Sometimes we use those words – "I'm busy" – when somebody asks us to do something we don't want to do. Oddly enough, being "busy" can be a form of procrastination. If we keep ourselves busy enough, we simply won't have to stop, look, and honestly evaluate our lives, to make the changes we know need to happen.

How many people do you know who, lying on a deathbed, would look back on his or her life and exclaim, "Gee, in retrospect, I wish I had been even busier"?

Fully Engaged

"Energy, not time, is the fundamental currency of high performance."

– Jim Loehr, performance psychologist
and best-selling author

Many people today live at a frantic pace. Their days are rushed, rapid fire and relentless – carved up into minutes and moments. They skim across the surface, alighting for seconds at dozens of destinations but rarely remaining for long at any one.

Most of us are just trying to do the best that we can. When demands upon our time exceed our supply, we make convenient choices that get us through our days and nights, but take a devastating toll over time. Most of us survive on too little sleep. We wolf down our meals, fuel up with expensive coffees, and stagger under the weight of it all. Faced with constant demands, we become quick-tempered and easily distracted. We return home from long days at work feeling exhausted and often see our families not as a source of joy and replenishment, but as one more demand upon an already overtaxed life.

Oddly enough, we even take pride in our ability to multi-task, and wear our willingness to put in long hours as a badge of honor. Starved for time, we cram as much as possible into every day. However, managing time efficiently is no guarantee you'll bring sufficient energy to whatever it is you're doing. Everything we do, from interacting with colleagues to making important decisions to spending time with family, requires energy. Without the right quantity, quality, focus, and force of energy, we are compromised in any activity we undertake. The ultimate measure of our lives is not how much time we spend, but how much energy we invest into the time we have.

Imagine a string of lights powered by one battery: you. The more lights in the string, the dimmer the glow from each bulb. As you slowly remove bulbs from the string, each subsequent bulb glows a little brighter. Remove enough bulbs and each light glows brilliantly. The challenge with life is deciding which bulb or task can be removed from the string. Many of us are reluctant to do so because we falsely believe admitting we're overwhelmed will make us appear weak or inadequate.

The first step in becoming fully engaged is to make a list of the activities/duties you perform on a daily, weekly, and monthly basis. You can make notes as you move through your day, keeping track of whether or not the task is work-related or one of your own choosing. Be fully engaged in this process and you'll begin to see patterns and processes at play. You may even discover that you're spending a tremendous amount of energy performing activities that are of minor importance. Look for ways to combine tasks and target time and energy-drainers. Initially, everything on your list may look vital, but stay with it and be honest. I recently heard someone complain about a crushing workload saying, "If it wasn't for that huge mortgage payment, I wouldn't work these extra hours." Consider whether keeping up appearances is playing a role in your busy life.

To be fully engaged, we must be physically energized, emotionally connected, mentally focused, and spiritually aligned with a purpose – whether grappling with a creative challenge at work, spending time with loved ones, or simply having fun. Performance, health, and happiness are grounded in the skillful management of energy and we have far more control over our energy than we realize.

All Work and No Play

"Life is what's happening when you're too busy to notice."

– Wayne Muller, author and speaker

The other day a friend called to ask me a question about her computer. She began the conversation with an apology.

"I know you're really busy," she said. "You probably don't appreciate having someone interrupting your day with a silly computer question."

I helped her resolve the computer problem and then stopped to reflect on the comment. We have all heard the expression, "All work and no play makes Jack (Jill) a dull boy (or girl)." Having quoted that idiom, let me state emphatically that I believe in becoming successful and pursuing my dreams. Yet too many people (myself included) are so focused on getting ahead that they drive themselves into the ground by working too much.

A couple weekends ago, my youngest son and I paid a visit to my mother at the family farm. We were only away for the weekend, but it was a great break and rejuvenated me so that I was ready to come back and work even harder on my projects. My question is this: will you enjoy some good down time? Your body needs it. Your mind needs it. Studies show that those who take regular breaks of refreshment and rest outperform those who work longer hours. It is all about quality time when it comes to work.

"I am so busy." We say this to one another as if our exhaustion were a trophy to place on the mantle, as though our ability to withstand stress is a mark of character. Often, the busier we are, the more important we see ourselves as being and (assume) the more impressive we must appear to others. To be unavailable to our friends and family, to be unable to find time for the sunset (or even to know the sun has set), to speed through our obligations without time for a single mindful breath, these have become the benchmarks for the successful life.

The truth is, the more our life speeds up, the more we feel weary, overwhelmed, lost. Our life and work rarely feel light, pleasant, or healing. Instead, as it all piles endlessly upon itself, the whole experience of being alive begins to melt into one huge obligation. Moreover, without rest, we lose our way. We miss the compass points that show us where to go, the nourishment that gives us comfort, the quiet that reveals our wisdom.

Studies suggest that over the last 25 years, our leisure time has declined by 37 percent while our workweek has increased by a full day. If you have difficulty relaxing when you have free time, your body is probably accustomed to running under pressure. It's time to start practicing new behaviors that reduce your reliance on adrenaline.

• Designate one day a week as a "no work" day – many people choose Sunday.

• Rejuvenate yourself. Enjoy a massage, a warm bath; listen to relaxing music; lose yourself in a good book, or do something outdoors.

• Take a brisk walk.

• Get a good night's sleep.

• Breathe deeply. When running on adrenaline, we tend toward shallow breathing.

When it comes to achieving success and living on purpose, rest and rejuvenation are vital to the process. Remember, all work and no play makes you a dull boy (or girl). Put aside some time for play. It will make your life more rewarding.

If Only … If Only

"Regret for the things we did can be tempered by time. It is regret for the things we did not do that is inconsolable."

– Sidney J. Harris, author, former
Chicago Sun-Times columnist

Bob was on fire, figuratively speaking. His job with the oil company had evolved to the point where he was now in charge of the crew and he drove his crew mercilessly.

Bob had a lovely wife who stayed home to care for the children. The family lived in a huge house and drove the best vehicles. Bob saw himself as a great provider. His wife saw him as an absentee husband and disengaged father. Bob's wife pleaded with him to take a break – not to work so hard – to spend more time with her and the children.

"You've got to make hay while the sun is shining!" said Bob, promising that there would be ample time for relaxing when he retired and plenty of cash to do it right!

The years flickered past and the children grew up. All the time, Bob's wife clung to the promise Bob had made to her: the promise of a rich, rewarding retirement together.

Eventually, Bob did retire an extremely wealthy man. To celebrate his retirement, he purchased a huge new motor home and said to his wife, "Now life really begins!"

On their first trip out of town – to visit the children Bob no longer knew – his wife suffered a heart attack and died. Bob cursed the unfairness of it all. Estranged from his children – lonely and world-weary – Bob grew bitter, resentful, overwhelmed with regret.

"If only,…" Bob whispered repeatedly. "If only."

Regretting is the act of revisiting past decisions or events, comparing them to what might have been, wishing they had been different, and suffering emotionally for it.

Hamilton Beazley, author of the book *No Regrets*, says regrets are inevitable. The question is if you will hold onto your regrets or let them go.

When I think of regret, I'm drawn to Robert Frost's poem *The Road Not Taken*. The poem begins with an intriguing question and the memorable phrase: "Two roads diverged in a yellow wood." The narrator chose "the one less traveled," a choice that "made all the difference." But what if he had chosen the well-traveled road? That choice, too, would have "made all the difference."

The road not taken is the source of all regrets. It seduces us with its fantasies of what might have been: limitless possibilities that would have unfolded for us "if only...."

Most of the regrets we have in life are little ones, and they're easy to let go. The more serious regrets are the challenge: a divorce, a lost job, the death of a partner or parent.

Regrets are a problem when we intensely or repeatedly revisit them. We re-experience the emotions the regrets generate and inflict tremendous damage to our self-esteem.

A wise friend once told me, "The only way to change the past is to change the present." In other words, make the best choices you can in this moment – at this time.

Looking at our regrets objectively can provide tremendous insight. Many of us can admit, "I've learned as much from what I've done wrong as from what I've done right."

When it comes to regret, we have two choices: hold onto them or let them go. When we consider our mistakes objectively and ponder their lessons, we can let go of regret and grow in our knowledge and, sometimes, wisdom. That's when the healing begins.

Releasing the Past

"We can draw lessons from the past, but we cannot live in it."
– Lyndon B. Johnson

There is no pill, lotion, potion, energy balancing, psychic reading, or affirmation that will change the past. Most, if not all, of the obstacles in our path to personal development are the result of unresolved experiences and issues from our past. The past can be a wonderful, empowering source of knowledge and inspiration – or a millstone we tie around our waist and drag behind us everyday. Are you dragging the past behind you?

When you think back over an experience, do you feel pain, regret, or anger? When you review a perceived failure, does that little voice in your head chastise you? You have surrounded that incident with emotional energy – energy that must be released.

Part of the pain associated with the past is the "if only" game. If only I had listened to my intuition. If only I had said, "I love you," before it was too late. If only I had said "no" instead of "yes" – "yes" instead of "no." But a mistake is just that: an error in judgment. Remember, we make our choices and decisions based upon the information available to us at the time. In other words, we did the best we knew how in that moment. We are not perfect and will make mistakes throughout our lifetime.

It may help to think of releasing the past in the following manner. Imagine yourself standing in a dark room. On the other side of the door is a room filled with sunshine. When you open the door the light streams into the dark room – the darkness does not overshadow the light. So it is within us. Releasing the past will bring light and peace to those dark places kept hidden deep inside. Guilt, shame, and blame fall into the category of dark places. We all have dark places that need light.

When emotions from the past begin to overwhelm you, stop, take a deep breath, and ask yourself the following questions. *Could* I allow myself to feel this emotion? *Will* I and *when*? Often, we don't feel our emotions, but suppress them, placing them in that great subconscious pressure cooker. Emotions we suppress do not go away, but continue to assert themselves – more aggressively each time. The resulting stress can be overwhelming both emotionally and physically. The answer to "When?" may be now, later today or in a few days time. If the answer is now, allow yourself to feel the emotion completely.

Now comes the crucial part: ask yourself, *could* I release this emotion? *Will* I and *when*? If the answer to "When?" is now, allow the emotion to dissipate. Close your eyes. Breathe deeply. It may help to visualize a great wind blowing the emotion away – perhaps seeing the emotion as dust, leaves, or snow. Visualizations are powerful; use one that works well for you. You may need to move through this process several times. Should the emotion return, repeat the process. You will soon discover that each time you do, the emotion is less potent, and the releasing process more effective.

Releasing the past can be a challenging yet immensely rewarding experience. As a result, you will become more aware of the love, harmony, and peace that surround you every day! Be courageous – the results will be worthwhile.

No Future in the Past

"Why can't I forget it? Can't I admit it? There ain't no future in the past."

– Vince Gill, singer-song writer

The patient looked distressed when the doctor entered the examination room.

"Is anything troubling you?" the doctor enquired.

"Yes," replied the patient. "I'm getting so forgetful. I can't remember where I park my car, where I'm going, or what I'm supposed to do when I get there. What should I do?"

The doctor pondered the question and then answered, "Pay me in advance."

Forgetfulness can be a good thing – especially when we forget pain from the past that threatens to impair the present. Now you might be thinking, "The past must be remembered – how else will we learn from it and keep from repeating it?" Correct, but why remember each time you felt pain? Why fill your mind with a detailed catalogue of past hurt? Remember instead the times that brought you joy or love. Unfortunately, those wonderful and magical moments too easily fade away when our focus is on the pain.

Mother Theresa once said, "If we really want to love, we must learn how to forgive." Forgiveness is a gift you give to yourself and a powerful way to release the past. Identify a situation from the past and ask yourself, "Am I willing to expend any more energy on this matter?" If the answer is "No," then let it go. Focus your energy on the healing, not the hurt. The same energy used to hold onto the past is the same energy you need to create a new and exciting life today – a life anchored in acceptance and unconditional love.

Keep in mind, it's not always necessary to inform the other individual for forgiveness or release to begin. In fact, it may be impossible to forgive someone face to face – the person may not even be alive. Don't let that stop you from releasing the anger and hurt.

Holding onto the anger, resentment, and a sense of betrayal can make your current life an unhappy one. When you forgive, you do it for you, not just for the other person. Let go of the past and release emotions that prevent you from growing emotionally. It's tough to have a loving and rewarding relationship with anyone else, much less yourself, if you continue to hold onto pain from the past. As best you can make peace with past love partners, your parents, children, your boss, or anyone who you think may have done you wrong. This can go a long way to improve your chances of a "healthy" relationship today. Be present in a new relationship by choosing to heal hurts and upsets of the past.

You *can* let go of the past and forgive. It takes strength to let go – forgiving takes moral courage. Forgiveness means accepting the lessons from the past and moving on.

A friend of Clara Barton, founder of the American Red Cross, asked her about a particularly traumatic event in her life. Miss Barton seemed at a loss.

"You don't remember it?" the friend queried.

Clara Barton replied, "I distinctly remember forgetting it."

Remember the past, learn from its lessons – but don't dwell upon the negatives, the pain, or the sadness. Be consumed by past joys and obsessed with gratitude. Remember the moments that lifted you up, the times you laughed and the memories of love and forgiveness shown to you by friends and family.

Letting Go of Success

"The past should be a springboard, not a hammock."

– Ivern Ball, author and motivator

Tom was livid. He'd been in to see his supervisor for the annual performance review. Tom was a salesperson and for many years, a tremendously successful one. As of late, however, his sales performance had been less than stellar. The supervisor needed Tom to meet his budgets. He needed Tom to be tremendously successful again.

"I had a million dollar year back in '96," fumed Tom. "I didn't let him forget it!"

Tom had been the young superstar and reveled in the glory. Now – to Tom – it seemed that history counted for little – that an accomplishment was only suitable for "glory days" conversations at the bar.

"There's no history anymore," Tom complained. "It's 'What have you done for me today?'"

Achievements need to be remembered and honored, but they also need to be released. Sometimes, we hold on so tightly to a past success that we stall our progress in the moment. I saw a great example of this in a recent workshop. The facilitator asked us to grasp a pen firmly in our right hand. He said our pen represented past success. He said, "Now, while holding on tightly to that past success, pick up another pen." We couldn't pick up anything else – that is, until we let go our grip on achievements.

Like you, I want to make the most of every day. And, like most people, I've long believed that the best way to do that is to let go of past failures.

But that's not all. You can never fully enjoy today while dwelling on past successes, either. People never succeed while resting comfortably on their laurels. As Sir William Osler said, "Live neither in the past nor in the future, but let each day's work absorb your entire energies, and satisfy your widest ambition."

Recently, I read a story about the actor Clark Gable. A friend paid Gable a visit one afternoon at the actor's home. She brought along her small son, who amused himself by playing with toy cars on the floor. He pretended he was racing those cars around a great track, which in reality was an imaginary circle around a golden statuette. The small statue the boy played with was actually the Oscar Gable won for his performance in the 1934 film, *It Happened One Night*.

When his mother told him the time had come to leave, the little boy asked the actor, "Can I have this?" pointing to the Oscar.

"Sure," he smiled. "It's yours."

The horrified mother objected. "Put that back immediately!"

Giving the child the golden statue, Clark Gable said, "Having the Oscar around doesn't mean anything to me; earning it does." The actor seemed to know that past success could be a comfortable hammock upon which he may be tempted to rest, rather than a springboard launching him to the next level.

Author L.P. (Leslie Poles) Hartley, put it this way, "The past is a foreign country; they do things differently there."

You may have learned to let go of past failures and mistakes in order to free the present. But will you loosen your grip on past successes and achievements in order to free the future?

"I like the dreams of the future better than the history of the past," said Thomas Jefferson.

I agree. After all, the future, not the past, is where the rest of your life will be lived.

The Path of Least Resistance

"All human problems arise from not accepting whatever is."

– Buddha

Mention the phrase, "the path of least resistance," and most people think they know of what you speak. However, there are at least two ways to view this concept.

One of the paths of least resistance is the path upon which your conditioning – your current belief system – leads you. You can follow this path with both eyes closed and with little thought as to where you're going. In fact, that's just how most people travel down this path: blindly doing what they've always done, wearing a rut in the terrain of their lives. This deep rut directs their path and keeps them safe from uncertainties of the unknown. There is little resistance on this path – simply because following it steers them clear of obstacles, challenges, and opportunities. This rut has become their comfort zone, and the only resistance they ever notice is when they veer off the path. For most people, fear of change keeps them firmly planted on this path of the familiar.

The second path of least resistance is one you actively choose when you set out to consciously move through a difficult or stressful situation. This is a deliberate path – one that comes with a lack of resistance and the acceptance of a difficult decision or activity.

Each situation – however challenging – has a path of least resistance. Too often, we spend our time complaining and resisting instead of accepting the reality of the current situation. The reality is we need to move through it, so let's start by accepting it.

Sometimes, we don't realize that we're in resistance. The other day I was enjoying a coffee with two friends. Rick and Susan (not their real names) got into a discussion about Rick's job. It seemed some new responsibilities had been added to Rick's plate. "Though I'm able to perform the added responsibilities well," Rick explained, "by the end of the day I'm exhausted and invariably suffering from a headache." Susan, a Reiki master, smiled and nodded. (Reiki is one of the more widely known forms of energy healing.)

"Your headache and exhaustion are the result of resisting the task at hand."

"The job needs to get done," Rick countered. "And I've accepted that responsibility."

"Accepting and resisting are two different things," explained Susan. She went on to tell us that we can consciously understand and accept the fact that a job has to be done and do it, yet still remain in a state of resistance. "You don't want to be doing the new task, but realize you have no option – so, you do it with a mood of opposition."

"Are you saying that I should simply resign myself to it?"

"No," said Susan. "Resignation would still leave you in a state of resistance."

By being in resistance, we put up roadblocks, which make the course more difficult. If we would simply accept the reality of the task, however daunting, then we could release the stress and move through the job following the path of least resistance. Resisting takes energy. It's like tying one arm behind our back, paddling upstream, climbing over the fence instead of walking through the gate. Try looking at each task as a challenge worthy of your best effort and derive a sense of accomplishment from a job well done.

Factor Number Two Summary: Reinforcement of Belief

Despite our best efforts, we find ourselves repeatedly in the same kind of unhealthy relationship or stressful financial situations – unable to break free of a patently destructive pattern of behavior. Our seeming inability to resolve these patterns – based on false beliefs and values – can be demoralizing and affect our self-worth.

Questions and statements pertaining to reinforcement of beliefs that you may wish to ponder by yourself or discuss as a group:

1. Do I find myself making the same mistakes repeatedly?
2. Do I perpetually find myself in the same situations or dysfunctional relationships?
3. Though I'm consciously aware of my tendency toward self-sabotage, I seem unable to break the pattern.
4. When I am judged as lacking or inadequate by others, I spiral down into a state of self-pity and hopelessness.
5. It seems to me that other people get all the breaks and I resent their success and happiness.
6. I feel my fears and inadequacies are uniquely mine and no one else truly understands how I feel or what I'm going through.
7. I seldom challenge my beliefs and am reluctant to investigate them further.
8. I often make statements that lack an element of self-responsibility as in, "That's just the way I am," or, "She pushes my buttons!"

Two Steps Forward

"To look backward for a while is to refresh the eye, to restore it, and to render it the more fit for its prime function of looking forward."

– Margaret Fairless Barber, English author

"Let's face it: you've been put in this world to do something wonderful with your life. You have a special purpose here on earth. And the starting point for realizing that purpose is self-management. It starts with accepting responsibility for yourself and everything you do so that you are moving progressively toward the realization of a worthy ideal."

– Murray Fuhrer, *Extreme Esteem*

Factor Number Three: Self-Responsibility

Albert Einstein once said, "The definition of insanity is doing the same thing over and over again expecting different results." Allow me to elaborate.

You walk down the street. There is a deep hole in the sidewalk. You fall in. You are lost. You are helpless. It isn't your fault. It takes forever to find a way out.

You walk down the same street. There is a deep hole in the sidewalk. You pretend you don't see it. You fall in again. You can't believe you are in this same place, but it isn't your fault. It still takes a long time to get out.

You walk down the same street. There is a deep hole in the sidewalk. You see it is there. You still fall in – your eyes are open but it's a habit. You know where you are. It is your fault. You get out immediately.

You walk down the same street. There is a deep hole in the sidewalk. You walk around it.

You walk down a different street.

This story aptly describes how many of us experience life. We all make mistakes. We all fall into traps and holes on our journey.

Sometimes the mistakes we make can be the result of not knowing any better. Other times – and perhaps more often – we are refusing to admit that what we've been doing simply isn't working. Oftentimes the behavior has become an unconscious habit that we just fall into (pun intended).

When you take an objective look at how you've lived your life, what themes or patterns do you notice? What streets do you continually go down and into what holes do you perpetually fall? What disempowering habits have you recognized, yet never changed? Whom have you blamed for the falls on your journey? What options or choices have you been denying?

Beliefs are something we accept as true, without question. We live our life around them, without thinking about them, questioning them or even being aware of them.

Holding on tight to self-limiting beliefs can prevent us from reaching our goals. If we won't or can't let go of such beliefs, we'll likely find ourselves doing the same things for years, falling into the same old holes, thinking that nothing will ever change. Sadly, nothing ever will, unless we can shake those self-imposed limitations.

We all come from different backgrounds, yet many of us share the same negative beliefs. To zero in on our negative programming, see if any of the following statements sound familiar.

I don't deserve happiness/success. It can't be done. It's too hard. I don't have the time. I'm not smart enough. My luck or my timing is always bad.

As a small child, you may have developed unbalanced or negative beliefs about yourself that actually helped you "fit in" to your family environment. At the time, these beliefs helped make sense of things that happened to you, things that would otherwise be very hard for you to accept. For example, if a small child is constantly ignored or neglected, one of his or her beliefs might be, "I am not worthwhile."

Those old beliefs and coping mechanisms may no longer be helping, but actually hindering you. My wish for you is that you become aware of the streets, the habits, and the behaviors that you engage in that are not in your best interest. Wayne Dyer says, "With awareness you have choice; with greater awareness, you have greater choice."

Being There Is Not Enough

"There's no greater sin than not being completely committed, not being completely there."

– Don Williams, country singer and songwriter

The last day of Grade 3 was a turning point for me. We were nearing the end of the day and the teacher was about to hand out report cards. We would soon find out whether or not we had passed into Grade 4. Our teacher, Mrs. T, started the report card ceremony by handing out small prizes for most consistent effort, most improved student, and the coveted perfect attendance award: a Swiss Army knife. I'd missed only one day of school the entire year (when a blizzard caused bus cancellations) and remained convinced the prize would soon be in my pocket. Besides, the winner had to be a boy – certainly, Mrs. T wouldn't award a Swiss Army knife to one of the girls.

Mrs. T held up the knife and announced with great enthusiasm, "The winner of this year's perfect attendance award is … (then she paused to build suspense) Allen." I felt deflated. Unlike most of us, Allen lived in town and only a few blocks from the school. He could attend class, even in the middle of a blizzard. Mrs. T congratulated Allen on his perfect attendance and added, "Allen was always in his seat when the bell sounded." Beaming, Allen accepted his prize, bowed to the class, and returned to his desk to examine the many gadgets.

Then something unexpected happened. Mrs. T handed out the reports cards and announced that, with one exception, everyone had passed. I flipped my card over. I had been promoted to Grade 4. Despite his perfect attendance, Allen had failed Grade

3. At that moment, I realized that just being there every day was not enough to ensure success.

I had a boss who once told me, "I don't reward people who just show up at work and keep a chair warm." To be "fully there" you have to be physically energized, emotionally connected, mentally focused, and spiritually aligned with a purpose beyond your immediate self-interest. Being "fully there" means feeling eager to get to work in the morning and just as happy to return home in the evening. It is a great day when we can fully immerse ourselves in work, family, and life – yet how often does that happen?

If we want to be fully there, we must draw upon four separate but related sources of energy: physical, emotional, mental and spiritual. They are interconnected and have a profound effect on each other. For example, to be physically fit yet emotionally troubled would not allow you to be completely in the moment. To be well balanced emotionally, yet physically exhausted to the point of collapse, would prove equally unproductive.

Let's be honest. We don't have an inexhaustible supply of energy and there are times – despite our best efforts – that we're not going to be completely in the moment. That's OK.

It's when "being there" becomes the exception rather than the rule that we run into problems. Succeeding in life and deriving as much enjoyment from each moment requires that we "live life on purpose," and that takes commitment and self-responsibility. If we are unwilling to be "fully there" in our work, with our friends and family – fully there in our life – we may one day arrive at a sad discovery: just being there every day was not enough.

Present, But Not Voting

"Many people die at 25 and aren't buried until they are 75."
– Benjamin Franklin, soldier, scientist, politician

My daughter Bethany loves to collect stories of the odd and unusual. And it's not unusual for her to drop into a chair next to me and announce, "Dad, listen to this weird story!" One such "weird" story involved philosopher Jeremy Bentham of London, England.

Bentham died in 1832 and left his estate to the University College London. He stipulated that his body be embalmed, dressed up and stored in a cabinet, calling it his "auto-icon." His mummy was kept at UCL, and, so the story goes, was brought in to preside over the annual meeting of university administrators. For years, the secretary of the board added to the minutes of each session, "Jeremy Bentham, present but not voting." Though he is no longer present at annual meetings, his preserved body is still displayed at the college.

I've known many people like Bentham: present, but not voting. They live without passion. They seem to have lost the thrill and wonder that comes from living life to the fullest. They get through each day, but no longer experience joy – no longer look forward to all that lies ahead. Alive? Yes, but not in full participation – present, but not voting.

As someone said, "No matter where you live, are you living where you are?" The challenge we all face today is finding time to live. Do you feel alive? Do you feel like you are living and enjoying life? On the other hand, are you numbed by job stress and the high demands of an over-booked schedule, seldom having time to enjoy some of life's simple pleasures?

If you find yourself in this category, it's time for a change. It's called "living each moment." Take time to smell the roses, look at the sunset, sit for a minute and listen carefully to the sounds around you. Hold hands with someone. We all know the drill, but I'll bet you're like most of us: cheating yourself out of those precious moments.

Dan Millman, author of *Way of the Peaceful Warrior*, described a time when his mentor, the man he referred to as Socrates, challenged him to sit out on a large, flat stone until he had "something of value" to share. Dan sat out on the rock for hours on end. On more than one occasion, believing he had come up with "something of value," he went to tell Socrates. Each time, Socrates decided the statement was of no consequence and he sent Dan back to the rock for more hours of pondering. Eventually, Dan had an insight that he knew was truly of value. When Dan shared this insight, Socrates looked up, smiled, and welcomed Dan back inside. The "something of value" that Dan had realized was this: "There are no ordinary moments."

This is the essence of being present – of being fully engaged – of living life to the fullest. No moment, nothing in life, should be taken for granted. In developing gratitude for every moment – for the simple joys, and even for the challenging times in our lives – we come to truly enjoy and appreciate life. Only then are we able to see the magic that surrounds us every second of every minute of every day.

Give yourself the gift of "living life to the fullest." Begin each day with gratitude. Be in the moment. Enjoy the moment. You will begin to see the magic of everyday life. You will be present – and voting.

Walking About Aimlessly

"This is our purpose: to make as meaningful as possible this life that has been bestowed upon us; to live in such a way that we may be proud of ourselves; to act in such a way that some part of us lives on."

– Oswald Spengler, German historian and philosopher

I receive many e-mails and, if you're like me, you don't have time to read them all: the funny little stories, the "off-color" jokes, and the "send this to six friends within seven minutes" chain letters. One I did read lately was entitled Unusual Laws. Some were so preposterous that I was left wondering what could ever have prompted their creation.

Here's one of my favorites: an ordinance in Dallas, Texas forbids "walking about aimlessly with no apparent purpose, lingering, hanging around, and lagging behind, idly spending time, delaying, sauntering and moving slowly about." I'm not sure how strenuously these laws have been enforced, but let's just say I'm glad that – at certain times in my life – I wasn't living in Dallas!

Then again, I wonder how many of us live life with "no apparent purpose, lagging behind, idly spending time, delaying" and generally "walking about aimlessly." In other words, how many of us are living without a clear direction, focus, and purpose? It is a mistake to think that moving fast is the same as actually going somewhere. As well, it is an error to believe that doing many things is as good as doing the right thing. People who are the most satisfied with their lives actually have somewhere to go and a plan to get there.

Author Mary Wollstonecraft Shelley – perhaps best known for her gothic horror novel, *Frankenstein* – put it this way: "Nothing contributes so much to tranquilizing the mind as a steady purpose – a point on which the soul may fix its intellectual eye."

News commentator Dan Rather had a vital question he would ask himself several times a day. In Rather's view, asking this one question (at a crucial time) helped him to become one of America's leading journalists. Rather wrote the question on three slips of paper. He kept one in his wallet, one in his pocket, and one on his desk.

The all-important question: "Is what you are doing now helping the broadcast?"

If the answer was yes, then he continued with his work, project, or idea. If the answer was no, then he stopped what he was doing and put his efforts into something else. Rather believed that if he did not focus his time and efforts constructively, he would end up in a job where his talents were underappreciated and his potential forever unrealized.

What if you were to ask yourself such a question several times a day? You might ask, "Is what I'm doing now helping me succeed?" or, "Is what I'm doing now helping me reach an important goal?" or, "Is what I'm doing now helping me grow?" I carry a note with me and it reads, "Am I making a difference today?"

Think seriously about your question. Choose a good one and then write it onto three small slips of paper or on the back of business cards. Carry one with you. Post one on your desk or computer monitor. You might even affix one to a prominent spot inside your vehicle.

Read your question several times a day. That one question will help you remain focused and, before you know it, you'll find yourself headed in the direction of your goals and desires. It's your choice – to walk with purpose and passion or risk landing behind bars in Dallas.

Follow the Follower

"Follow the path of the unsafe, independent thinker. Expose your ideas to the dangers of controversy. Speak your mind and fear less the label of "crackpot" than the stigma of conformity. And on issues that seem important to you, stand up and be counted at any cost."

– Thomas J. Watson, founder of International Business Machines (IBM)

Dr. Robert Anthony, best-selling author and motivational speaker, once said, "The opposite of bravery is not cowardice but conformity." Tallulah Bankhead, the outrageous, outspoken "Dahling" of early films once quipped, "Nobody can be exactly like me. Sometimes even I have trouble doing it." Nonetheless, most of us do have trouble being ourselves – especially in a world that wants us to conform.

One of the deepest desires of young people, especially teens, is to be accepted by their peers. Like all of us, they want to feel valued. It's during these critical teenage years, according to Earl Nightingale, that we begin to play a game called "Follow the Follower." The game should not be confused with "Follow the Leader." Following the follower is about conforming: talking, dressing, acting and thinking like one another, everyone following everyone else.

The other day a good friend, Kevin, shared with me an experience he had outside a local convenience store. A group of young men had congregated near the entrance to the business, dressed in a manner that would dissuade most people from approaching them. Not Kevin, however. He went up to the group, introduced himself, and asked one of the young men why he chose to dress in such a manner. The lad studied Kevin with narrowing eyes then replied, "Because I don't want to be like everyone else."

Kevin looked at the other group members – all dressed the same.

"So, you want to be unique, original, one-of-a-kind?"

The young man nodded and the group concurred.

"But you all look exactly the same," he pointed out. "Exactly like everyone else."

The group was silent.

In adulthood, we discover who we really are and do our best to grow into that person. We find our value not in acceptance by others, but because we believe in our worth. It's a wonderful day when we can honestly say, "I know who I am and I'm glad to be me."

Children's author Dr. Seuss got it right when he wrote, "Be who you are and say what you feel, because those who mind don't matter and those who matter don't mind." It takes strength to oppose the crowd. It takes courage to speak up for what you believe. It takes faith to act upon your intuition. Ultimately, your success will always be a result of being true to yourself rather than a carbon copy of somebody else.

We all have heroes – people we admire and emulate. Recognizing the finer qualities of others and choosing to become more courageous, passionate, decisive, enlightened and such is admirable. However, at the end of our life, the question we never want to face is, "Why couldn't you have just been you?"

In every society, there is a need – indeed, a necessity – to conform to certain laws and rules of moral conduct. When I speak of being truly you, I do not mean justifying addictions or patterns of self-destructive behavior. Consider the lack of self-responsibility in the statement, "That's just who I am."

Whatever your dreams, whatever your aspirations, your greatest success will come from your being the best *you* possible. In a world that wants you to conform, choose instead to be unlike anyone else – choose to be *you*. It's a challenging and rewarding job and no one can do it as well as you.

Painted with a Different Brush

"Tis the business of little minds to shrink; but he whose heart is firm, and whose conscience approves his conduct, will pursue his principles unto death."

– Thomas Paine, pamphleteer, revolutionary, radical intellectual, and deist.

My cousin loved the color orange. In his home, he had orange wallpaper, orange carpeting, orange furniture, and orange drapes. I bet his bed had an orange comforter. If he could have found orange appliances, he probably would have installed them, too. His fine wife tolerated his obsession with orange and made certain the home was always tasteful despite the predominant shade. Occasionally, my cousin would wear an orange T-shirt and joked that he was in camouflage.

Sometimes it's good to blend into your surroundings. Other times, it's better to stand out from the crowd. In his popular book, *Deciding How To Live*, motivational speaker and writer, Steve Goodier shares the following story about an armored truck that toppled on a Miami overpass and rained more than half a million dollars onto the street below.

"Police said that witnesses reported seeing rush-hour commuters loading money into their cars and driving off while two

Brinks workers lay bleeding on the street. Police had pleaded with residents to return the money, but got nothing but laughter until a mother and a boy came forward. A mother came to the police and spilled out cash and coins totaling $19.53. A young boy turned in 85 cents. After two days, they were the only people to return money scooped up from the armored truck."

In a city that seemed to think alike, two people had a different idea. They were not painted with the same brush as everyone else.

"I have six children," said the mother, "and I needed to set a good example."

She could certainly have used a little extra cash to supplement her low retail store wage. She chose not to blend into her surroundings.

The boy who turned in 85 cents did so because he felt, "It was wrong for me to keep anything" (that didn't belong to him). He too stood out from the crowd.

These two people – who just wanted to do the right thing – set an example that others will never forget. These two people demonstrated their values. Most people talk about values: what they believe to be right or wrong. But whether or not we realize it, we all *live* our true values. Our actions, more than our words, will show what we truly believe. Living your values means that your words match your actions, which, in turn, match your beliefs. Clarifying what really matters to you, knowing what you stand for, will set you free to live life to its fullest.

If you don't know who you are, you can't be true to yourself. Sounds obvious, but many of us go through life without taking the time to identify what truly matters. Imagine an airplane that went wherever the wind took it. Who knows where it would eventually land? And the flight itself would likely be stressful and uncertain.

Clarifying your values and then living in harmony with those values provides you with an inner peace and tranquility that allows you to move confidently through life. It allows you to stop mechanically reacting and start consciously responding. We always know when we're not living our values: we experience a vague sense of uneasiness and we react defensively.

Do you blend with your surroundings or do you live your values and stand out from the crowd? If so, paint yourself fortunate.

Why Don't You Watch Where I'm Going?

"We've gotten to the point where everybody's got a right and nobody's got a responsibility."

– Newton Minow, Chairperson of the Federal Communications Commission

Some time ago, my wife and I were driving through our neighborhood enjoying a quiet conversation when two teenage boys on BMX bikes shot across the street in front us. I tromped on the brakes, skidding to a halt less than a meter away from the two. "Hey!" yelled the larger of the two boys, shaking his fist at me. "Why don't you watch where I'm going?"

"Yeah," spat the smaller lad, "His brakes don't work!" The two then darted off down a back alley. We were both shaken and our quiet drive was over.

How many people do you know who go through life with the same attitude?

"Why don't you watch where *I'm* going – *my* brakes don't work!"

To achieve a healthy level of self-esteem, you must be able to accept who you are and be confident about your decisions and behavior. However, there is another component of self-esteem that is often overlooked: the ability to take responsibility for our actions.

Since being responsible requires effort and a number of difficult decisions, many people convince themselves that it is a hopeless task. Some blame others for their problems. Others hope that someone will come along and make everything all right. You cannot respect or trust yourself if you pass on to others the burden of your existence.

Self-responsibility determines satisfaction and success in all areas of our lives. In personal relationships, people who are content go beyond saying, "I want... ." They ask, "What am I willing to do to get what I want?" They pay attention to the quality of the time they spend with loved ones. They notice whether communication between parties is clear, are sensitive to the feelings of others, face challenges and deal with conflicts.

Self-responsibility means being aware of boundaries – recognizing what is appropriate in a given situation and acting accordingly. We've all been in situations where someone said or did something that left us astounded by its inappropriateness. The principle of self-responsibility entails a profoundly important moral idea. Taking responsibility for our own existence implies respect for other people – the recognition that they do not exist simply to satisfy our needs. We are not entitled to treat others as means to our own ends or to take their contributions for granted – and we should not tolerate such treatment.

Self-responsibility should not be confused with taking inappropriate responsibility for others. We're not helping anyone when we solve problems for others that they can and should solve on their own. We're merely contributing to a lack of responsibility.

One of the most useful tools for moving toward the goal of self-responsibility is to ask the following question in as many situations as possible: "If I was totally self-responsible right now, what would I be doing?" In most cases, you will know the answer. It's just a matter of listening to the response and acting upon it. If you ask yourself this question and think about the answer several times a day, you will find yourself developing the type of awareness that leads to self-responsibility.

Although total and consistent self-responsibility may not at all times be achievable, we can learn to operate more self-responsibly if we become aware of the issue and take it seriously. Accept the challenge – fix your faulty brakes and stop expecting others to watch where you're going.

Bad Luck or Bad Choices

"It is our choices that show what we truly are, far more than our abilities."

– J. K. Rowling, author of the Harry Potter series

I remember the day. I was venting to a friend about my sad state of affairs: too many bills, too little income, too much stress, too little sleep. My friend listened intently and when I had finished complaining, made the comment, "Gee, if it wasn't for bad luck you wouldn't have any luck at all." That stopped me in my tracks. Was I being plagued by bad luck? If so, why? I pondered the statement for some time and slowly came to the sad realization that the majority of my "bad luck" was the result of my bad choices.

Let me explain.

If you buy a new vehicle, keep it up with regular maintenance and run over a nail on the way to work resulting in a flat tire, that's bad luck. However, if you drive on your tires until they're bald, don't bother to have them balanced, or check the tire pressure, and then the tire goes flat, that's not bad luck, but bad choices. The tire failed because you chose not to buy a new set. The tire failed because you chose *not* to have them balanced or take time to check the tire pressure.

It's bad luck if you leave your house on vacation and, while you're away, there's a torrential downpour, causing the sewer to back up and flood your basement. It's a bad choice not to care for your house – replacing the shingles, fixing the windows, servicing the furnace, repairing the wiring – until it becomes a run-down heap.

It's bad luck to be let go from a company that downsizes. It's a bad choice to arrive late for work everyday, dress like a slob, gossip about co-workers, and have a negative attitude, resulting in your termination.

If you choose to associate with shady characters or frequent dicey establishments, and you are assaulted and robbed, is that bad luck or bad choices?

You get the point.

How often do we call something bad luck when it is really the result of bad choices?

At the heart of this issue is self-responsibility – taking ownership of our lives and actions. Are you taking full responsibility for your life and choices?

I know of a friend who recently found himself in desperate financial straits. His unsecured debt – credit cards and the like

– was out of control. After much effort, he was able to secure a consolidation loan and begin a repayment routine. Half way through the term of the loan, he had accumulated a new debt nearly equal to the original amount. The resulting financial burden brought on a depression for which he began taking medication.

What about you? Do you experience bad luck or bad choices?

The next time you hear someone say, "He is having a run of bad luck," perhaps you ought to counter with, "Or is he reaping the result of bad choices?" And when people say, "Good luck seems to follow you," you can smile and nod, knowing that you make your own good luck. The more seriously you consider your choices and their consequences, the more adept you'll become at making the right, wise, and good choices.

It has been my experience that people who make good choices tend to experience good luck. So, if you want a little good luck, make some good choices.

Myth of the Perfect Job

"About 90 to 95 percent of all people work at jobs which are unfulfilling and which they dislike and would leave in a minute if they only knew what they really wanted to do."

– Sidney Madwed, writer, speaker, motivator

"I want a job I enjoy, where I'm treated with respect, and paid a decent wage."

Danny and I were talking about jobs, our shared experiences as employees, and our expectations of an employer. Danny had been laid off recently and was clearly upset.

"Am I asking too much?" Danny stared off into space. "I don't think so."

The conversation sent my mind casting back to a time when I was in search of the "eternally" perfect job. That one place where I would *forever* feel contented, respected by my colleagues and management, where my talents were recognized, appreciated, and rewarded financially – a nirvana where I liked everyone and everyone liked me. At that period of my life, the moment I encountered any persistent negativity, criticism, or (heaven forbid) someone who didn't like me, I was off again – usually every two to five years – onto another city, another province, another leg in my quest.

Over time, I realized that rewarding careers develop over time, after months and even years of on-the-job experience and by learning to deal with a variety of situations and people. Even the most exciting, fulfilling job has its occasional downside. In other words, there's no such thing as the "eternally" perfect job.

Let's be realistic. Some jobs simply pay the bills; it's something we do until we can do what we want. Other jobs become lifelong careers. Sometimes people start a new career with high hopes. Things fall into place and they accept what seems to be their dream job. Then a few years later, they're dissatisfied. Did they do something wrong?

The answer may be no. Each of us is an evolving individual: growing, learning, and honing our skills. With some jobs, there simply comes a time when you outgrow your surroundings and require greater challenges, new experiences, and a fresh perspective. Any number of factors can affect your willingness to get out of bed and head to work. Maybe it's the annual budget report you have to prepare or the angry client you have to appease. It could be the hectic times that leave you feeling overwhelmed or the slow stretches when time seems to stand still. A difficult co-worker or the stress of a new manager can also turn things unpleasant.

Few things will affect your self-esteem as much as working daily at a job you absolutely despise. What you need to determine is whether the things upsetting you at your job are reasons to start circulating your resume. These are some key questions to ask.

• Do you still enjoy the core activities of your job? If the focus of the job is helping people and you spend more time doing paperwork, perhaps focusing on the satisfaction you get from working with people will help buoy your enthusiasm.

• Is this a temporary situation? Are things in upheaval because of a budget cut or a temporary personnel shortage? Will this issue be resolved in the near future?

• Are there measures you can take to improve the situation, short of leaving? Can you ask for help from your co-workers or manager to make the situation tolerable?

• Have you shared your concerns and – most importantly – your expectations with your employer? None of us is a mind reader. You may be surprised by the response.

If you're unhappy with your job, make sure to determine why. You might require a simple adjustment rather than a change. An open airing of concerns, a review of expectations, or even a short vacation can turn unfulfilling work into a job you enjoy.

What Do You Want to Be (When You Grow Up)?

"When you find what you love to do, you'll also find the rocket fuel you'll need to propel you past the obstacles you'll have to overcome to make your dream happen."

– Pat Lynch, author, speaker, originator of the phrase, "Thinking outside the box"

I was having coffee with a friend the other day when the topic shifted from work and family to finding our dream and pursuing our purpose.

"I still don't know what I want to be when I grow up," he said with a chuckle and then added after a long pause, "Maybe I don't want to know."

What do you want to be when you grow up?

"What," of course, turns out to be the number one question in life. What do you want to be? The answer to that one simple question has baffled most of us for a very long time.

It may surprise you to learn that most people know what "it" is, but won't admit it.

Psychologist, Abe Mazlow called it the "need to know and the fear of knowing."

This simply means that most of us are dying to know what "it" is, but we don't really want to know because if we do, we'll have to take responsibility for it and act on it. So our ego – that false part of us that's usually in charge and determined to look good at any expense – decides it's best not to know.

One of the biggest reasons most us have trouble finding our purpose is because we're looking for it in terms of what's "possible, reasonable, responsible, and realistic." You see, it's not about more of the same (same perspective, same strategy), just harder – it's what you can do, what you're here to do – what you're meant to share with the world!

Would you like to find your dream and discover your purpose? Start by asking yourself some questions and write (yes, write) down your answers. That makes them real and the more real they are, the more certain they are to happen. Let's begin:

- What do you love to do?
- What would you do even if you weren't being paid to do it?
- What do you get lost in doing and lose all track of time?
- What do you do that gives you energy?
- If you weren't afraid, what would you do?

Now ask yourself: What did you love to do when you were a kid? Chances are that's when you had a clearer idea of who you were and what you wanted to be.

Just make sure your dream meets three simple criteria: first, that it's what you crave; second, that it's specific, tangible and measurable; and third, that it's big enough! Unless your dream's bigger than your comfort zone and larger than your current life, it won't have the power you need to turn you on and move you to the next level.

Why hasn't your dream happened already? Why haven't you discovered your passion?

We unknowingly put a limit on how good we'll let things become before we slam on the brakes and begin sabotaging the very success we've worked so hard to achieve.

Talk with older people and they'll tell it to you straight: more often than not, what they regret most is what they *didn't* do, the risks not taken, the dreams not pursued.

Decide now: will you refuse to give up, quit, sell out, wimp out, play it safe, let others run your life, do as you're told or do anything else that turns your life into a giant void?

After you've finished reading this column, get a pen and paper and write in bold letters, "Yes! I'm going to start making my dream happen today!"

Perception is Not Reality.

"Man has always sacrificed truth to his vanity, comfort, and advantage. He lives by make-believe."

– W. Somerset Maugham, English playwright, novelist, and short story writer

The other day, someone told me that perception is reality. Sorry, but in my view, perception is *not* reality. Reality is reality. Perception is reality filtered through our beliefs, values, and past experiences.

Eckhart Tolle in *The Power of Now* says, "To meet everything and everyone through stillness instead of mental noise is the greatest gift you can offer to the universe." Tolle challenges us to become the "Witness" – the watcher of our feelings – the observer of our thoughts and sensations. Our beliefs, decisions, opinions, and emotional states are shaped chiefly by what we might refer to as the "Reactor." The Reactor resides at the other end of the spectrum from the Witness. As the Witness observes, the Reactor reacts.

We are conditioned to be reactionary, partly because our culture demands that we react quickly to the ever-changing circumstances of our environment. He who hesitates is lost. Therefore, we make decisions "on the fly" as we cruise through our frantic day. Sometimes it's necessary to be reactionary. We must trust our intuition and our reflexes. If a fire has broken out in your home, you must act quickly to get to safety. There won't be time to sit and think things through. The Reactor can save our lives.

However, when it comes to our emotions, attitudes, and beliefs, living as the Reactor has its consequences. By constantly "reacting" we can damage our relationships with others, sabotage our efforts to succeed and thrive, thereby perpetrating destructive, dysfunctional cycles of behavior and belief. Being reactionary becomes habitual with little reinforcement. When in

Witness mode, we see these cycles at work and learn new ways of functioning outside of them. A switch is thrown between that moment of feeling a sensation and becoming identified with the sensation. That switch is thrown automatically most of the time. Being the Witness means we can actually see it being thrown. We feel the sensation, we note the emotions and then we stop, become quiet, and investigate our thinking.

By being the Witness, we empower ourselves to function at a much higher level of awareness than when we are the Reactor – we step beyond our initial perceptions. The chief benefit to perfecting this Witnessing stance is that we can be *responsive* rather than *reactionary*. We open ourselves to a new world of opportunity and see a vast array of choices we can make about how we respond to people and circumstances in our environment. We see connections and patterns in our lives that emerge as we mindfully witness life. Moreover, for the first time, we awaken to the fact that we truly do create our own realities by our thoughts, feelings, and perceptions.

It takes practice, attention, and mindful persistence to recondition the mind to function this way. It requires strength, dedication and bravery. As a coach, I suggest you take the time to listen to what your heart is saying. Be still. Be quiet. Sit, walk, and run. Meditate, pray. Journal, read. Learn. Whatever it takes! Truly listen to your heart and get to know yourself. You'll see the reality beyond mere perception.

The transformation that takes place when you decide to be the Witness can be quite remarkable! You become more aware – more confident. You begin to understand your motivations and face your fears. The greatest reward of all is that you begin to see the reality and truth of life, people, and situations – not simply your perception of it. And with that knowledge comes a greater sense of understanding and inner peace.

Perception is reality. I think not.

Adjust Your Thermostat

"We have no right to ask when adversity comes, 'Why did this happen to me?' unless we ask the same question for every moment of happiness that comes our way."

– Unknown

The other day, I was sitting in front of my computer monitor, pondering a new column. On this particular day the sky was overcast, a wintry breeze circled the house, and it felt like rain. The furnace had just come on to chase the damp chill from the house. As I wandered into the kitchen for a coffee, I glanced through the window at the thermometer. Five degrees Celsius. As I walked back to my office, I noticed the digital thermostat on the living room wall. The preset room temperature was 19 degrees. Obviously, the temperature in the house had dropped below the preset and engaged the furnace.

Back in front of my monitor, I began to think about the difference between thermometers and thermostats. Both measure temperature, but the thermometer does nothing about it. You might say a thermometer is a passive device while the thermostat is an active one. They both experience the same variable, but only a thermostat responds.

Some people are like thermometers: they passively note damaging factors in their life, but do nothing to change the situation. They have problems and difficulties, yet believe there isn't anything they can do about it. They feel helpless as they watch life happen to them. At the core of this belief is a certain lack of self-responsibility. Others are more like thermostats. When they are faced with adversity, they step up to the plate and start swinging. They believe that something can and should be done – a solution can be found and a hurt can be healed. They respond, they make decisions, they go into motion. They accept responsibility for changing their current situation.

Now you might say a thermometer is not designed to react – it's simply incapable of doing or responding. Point well taken, but how many people do you know who are fully and completely capable of responding, yet simply choose not to? They believe that – like the thermometer – they simply are incapable of making a difference.

In his best selling book, *Joy along the Way*, writer and motivational speaker Steve Goodier refers to a comment made some years ago by advice columnist Ann Landers. Ann had been asked, "What would be the single most useful bit of advice you could share with all of humanity?" After some consideration, Ann replied, "Expect trouble as an inevitable part of life. When it comes, hold your head high, look it squarely in the eye, and say, 'I will be bigger than you. You cannot defeat me.'" In other words, respond courageously and creatively. Accept responsibility for changing your current situation.

If we are to accept Ann's assertion as correct, then we must make a conscious decision to be bigger than any trouble that comes our way. If you've become stuck in your current situation because you feel frightened or helpless, it's time to respond. It's time to make a decision. It's time to go into motion. When you become bigger than your problem, it cannot defeat you. Choose to respond – to be an active participant in your life.

Today and everyday, be a thermostat and not a thermometer. When life sends a chill your way, respond to the uncomfortable situation with action. You may discover that life is a lot more comfortable as you warm up to the idea of a self-responsible existence.

Be the Change

"Be the change you wish to see in the world."

– Mahatma Ghandi

The other day someone asked me why I devoted so much time and energy to teaching and speaking on the topic of self-esteem. Besides the fact that I feel most alive and "on purpose" when I'm writing and speaking on the theme, I have a burning desire to change the world. That may sound pretentious, but I believe we can all play a role in changing the world.

I know what you're thinking and you're right. You don't change lives. People have to take your words and apply them in order for change to result. The truth is making a difference in the world does not require playing the roles of a diplomat, politician, policy-maker, or even a warrior. It does require a willingness to build bridges of understanding with other people. A kind word of encouragement, a gentle touch, the unselfish sharing of your time and talents all contribute to making the world a better place. When you change your attitude, everything around you changes with it.

Perhaps you have a radical idea – something that's never been done before. "If something has not been done before," says Kofi Annan, former Secretary General of the United Nations, "it does not mean it can't be done, only that you could be the first to do it."

Thom Hartmann is an award-winning, best-selling author, and the host of a nationally syndicated daily radio talk show. In his leading work entitled *Constantly Changing the World*, Thom shares an intriguing story a Cree Native American storyteller and teacher told him: "According to my tradition, from the beginning of creation, every morning, when the sun comes up, we are each given four tasks by our Creator for that day. First, I must learn at least one meaningful thing today. Second, I must teach at least one meaningful thing to another person. Third, I must do something for some other person, and it will be best if that person does not even realize that I have done something for them. And, fourth, I must treat all living things with respect."

What a simple, yet powerful formula to bring about change – both personally and with everyone you encounter. Change begins with a choice. Robert Frost understood this when he wrote, "Two roads diverged in a wood, and I … I took the one less traveled by, and that has made all the difference."

Just as our faces mirror our inner spirit, so does our belief system influence our every thought, word, and deed. What is your belief system based on? Are you able to forgive or love others? Have you been forgiven or loved yourself? Perhaps the first change that needs to happen is to change the way you see yourself and the world around you.

Look at your life. How would you describe it? Fulfilling, exciting, moving forward? Or rushed, stressful, and sliding backward? There are things we dream of doing one day and deeds we wish we could forget. As with everything in life, every small and seemingly insignificant step counts.

Change in the hearts and minds of individuals can bring great and far-reaching results. I challenge you: carry an inner will and courage to make a difference and become an agent of change. Travel the road that is less traveled and far less sought.

Serious Wrecks

"You must do the thing you think you cannot do."

– Eleanor Roosevelt

As a teenager, one of my favorite haunts was the local auto salvage yard. Ed, the owner, was content to let me roam the rows of wrecks, confident that I would use my good sense and stay out of trouble. For whatever the reason – morbid curiosity, perhaps – the serious wrecks held the greatest fascination for people. These were vehicles involved in head-on collisions, rollovers, and such – often with fatalities. These vehicles could not be salvaged for parts, so were parked in the back of the yard for crushing. Without exception, each "wreck" was the result of a momentary lapse of good judgment: someone passed on a solid line, drove too fast, drove while impaired, failed to stop at an intersection, or simply did not pay attention to the road or drive for the conditions.

As I grew up, I discovered a lapse of good judgement in life could also result in a serious emotional wreck. Sometimes, the wreck had nothing do with our "lack of judgement" but the poor, cruel, or foolish choice of another, leaving us to deal with the aftermath. I began to wonder why certain people could experience an emotional "head-on" and survive it while others, having endured (what seemed to me) an incident of far less emotional magnitude, were utterly destroyed.

In the mid-'80s, I had the good fortune to meet John Walsh, host of North America's Number 1 crime-fighting show, *America's Most Wanted.* His incredibly successful career, as host of a nationally televised program and an advocate for victim's rights, was a career Walsh never anticipated.

In the summer of 1981, Walsh was living the American dream. He and his wife, Reve, had a beautiful six-year-old son, Adam, the joy of their lives. But that joy was shattered on July 27th, 1981, when Adam was abducted and later found murdered.

The question was posed to Walsh, "How were you able to rebound from such a devastating experience?" I don't recall John's exact words, but the essence of his response was this: in the midst of the anger, enormous loss, and sorrow, he realized he could still make a choice. He could allow Adam's death to destroy him and his family, thus adding another victim to the police report. Alternatively, he could honor Adam's memory by surviving. Walsh chose the second option. Because of that choice, he made a tremendous difference to the world. He was chosen by *CBS Portraits* as one of the One Hundred Americans Who Changed History.

Have you ever seen two people experience the same event or situation, but respond in two completely different ways? Some time ago, I was at a seminar where a simple formula was taught, and it has stuck with me for many years. I've found so many applications for it that I frequently use it in my own training. It is this: E + R = O (Event, plus Response, equals Outcome). We cannot control the events that happen in life, but we can control our responses, and therefore, to some degree, the outcome.

Will a great attitude make everything in your life work out the way you want it to? Some positive-thinking gurus might have you think that, but I don't believe it. I do believe, however, that a positive attitude helps you to frame a positive response, which influences a positive outcome, no matter what the circumstances.

It's difficult sometimes when you're in the thick of things, to realize how much of an impact your response can have on the outcome of any situation. When you find yourself reacting emotionally or negatively to a situation that comes your way, ask yourself these questions: Do I have a choice in how I will respond to this situation? Which choice will lead to a more positive outcome?

Keeping that simple formula (E + R = O) in front of you can be a helpful way to remind yourself that you do have power over the outcome of difficult circumstances.

Charles Swindoll put it this way: "The remarkable thing is we have a choice every day regarding the attitude we will embrace for that day. We cannot change our past, we cannot change the fact that people will act in a certain way. We cannot change the inevitable. The only thing we can do is play on the one string we have, and that is our attitude. I am convinced that life is 10 percent what happens to me and 90 percent how I react to it."

Self-Management

"The story of the human race is the story of men and women selling themselves short."

– Abraham Maslow, psychologist and originator of the *Hierarchy of Needs*

I grew up on a dairy farm. Those of you familiar with the business know it's not an occupation – it's a lifestyle. Up every morning at five for morning milking, back at five in the afternoon for evening milking. In between, you farm.

Everything revolved around the milking of the cows. We seldom took a vacation – few people were willing to milk our 40 cows twice a day. If we went to town (about once a week), we couldn't stay for a movie or late dinner. We had to be home by five and we were – seven days a week, 365 days a year.

Now don't get me wrong – it was a good life and a great experience. It taught me dedication, self-responsibility, and the value of hard work. I wouldn't trade those days for anything and I'd be less than honest if I said there weren't times when I wish I were still a kid on the farm. We used to refer jokingly to dad as "Dah Boss." He was quick to defer to my mother who would each time counter with, "The cows are in charge, not us." My parents were farmers – fine examples of entrepreneurship.

I think one of the great tragedies in life is that most of us are brought up to think of ourselves as employees rather than employers, as entrepreneurs. This attitude is a major cause of unhappiness and underachievement in life. The myth of the employee leads people to see themselves as helpless and dependent upon "the company." From an early age, we look for someone to provide us with work to do and the money we need to live.

Many of us settle for far less than we're capable of achieving and can't understand why we feel so dissatisfied and frustrated with life. The truth is, we have an inborn drive toward the realization of our full capability. A force within drives us onward and upward toward the achievement of our dreams and desires. Some people attempt to stifle that "drive" by drinking too much alcohol, watching too much television, socializing too much, and even resorting to drugs and dangerous behavior. But it will not be stifled.

Let's face it: you've been put in this world to do something wonderful with your life. You have a special purpose here on earth. And the starting point for realizing that purpose is self-management. It starts with accepting responsibility for yourself and everything you do so that you are moving progressively toward the realization of a worthy ideal.

In self-management, you accept the fact that you are self-employed. You work for yourself. No matter who signs your paycheck, no matter if you've worked for a company all your life, you are always self-employed – the president of your own service corporation. You are an independent entrepreneur, selling services to your company.

When you accept the fact that you are in charge of your working destiny, you begin to realize that self-management is the vehicle that will take you from wherever you are to where you want to be. You're not a passenger – you're the driver. You determine your own destiny. You're not subject to the whims and fancies of fate and corporate circumstance.

Take some time now and get comfortable with the idea that you are "Dah Boss."

What Do You Need?

"Everything you need, you already have. You are complete right now; you are a whole, total person, not an apprentice person on the way to some place else. Your completeness must be understood by you and experienced in your thoughts as your own personal reality."

– Beverly Sills, the Coloratura Soprano

Making a living as a full-time professional writer often means accepting freelance work. By freelance, I mean contracting to do a specific project for a business or individual: a brochure, newspaper or magazine article, even editing a manuscript. I recall some years back working on a series of press releases for a business engaged in event promotion. I ignored the red flags that popped up during the initial meeting when the client scribbled some notations onto a pamphlet and then tossed it across the desk to me.

"Make something up from this," he said and turned back to his work. I went home, read the pamphlet, and made a list of questions. When I called the next day, the response was less than favorable. "I don't have time to deal with this right now," was the reply. "That's why I hired you!"

He instructed me to put some sample releases together and then fax him back. He would review the samples and let me know if any changes were required. I did just that: put together two sample releases and a proposal for the balance. When the client called me back, I was told the releases were completely unacceptable. I had – apparently – missed the entire point.

Frustrated now, I said, "I don't understand what you need!"

To this, the client snapped, "I don't either – but I *will* when I see it!"

Do you know what you need? I'm not speaking of material things like a bigger house, newer car, or more money. What do you need to live a rich, full, vibrant life?

Stephen Covey, author of *The 7 Habits of Highly Effective People*, says all people share four basic needs: the need to live, to love, to learn, and to leave a legacy.

We need to live. Not just to breathe or survive day to day, but to live our lives fully. Philip Humbert, recognized writer, speaker, and life coach, asks, "What remarkable, extraordinary, and amazing things will you do with this wild and wonderful miracle, your one and only life?" What a great question. Do you have a great answer?

We need to love but we also need to *be* loved. Margaret Mead, the outspoken American anthropologist, perhaps said it best when she declared, "One of the oldest human needs is having someone wonder where you are when you don't come home at night."

We need to learn – not only for a few years when we're young and going to school, but for our entire time here on earth. We must be committed to life-long learning – learning that never ceases, learning that becomes our passion. There's truth in the old assertion, "When we stop learning, we stop living."

Finally, we need to leave a legacy. I'm not speaking of money or property bequeathed to another by will. I'm speaking of the basic desire to want our lives to count for something.

In the words of Ralph Waldo Emerson, "To leave the world a little bit better, whether by a healthy child, a garden patch or a redeemed social condition; to know even one life has breathed easier because you have lived. This is to have succeeded."

Will you only know what you need when you see it? Or will you decide here and now what you need and pursue it?

Living with Integrity

"Integrity is one of several paths – it distinguishes itself from the others because it is the right path, and the only one upon which you will never get lost."

– M.H. McKee, writer and philosopher

How often do you daydream about living a better life – a life that more accurately reflects your true values and deepest desires? How many times have you come to the end of a busy week and flirted with the idea of packing a bag and leaving it all behind?

Are you the person you say you are? Do your words reflect your actions? Are little white lies keeping you from experiencing true happiness? Are you living with integrity?

You might think integrity simply means being honest and true to your word coupled with the adherence to a moral code. That's certainly part of it, but integrity also means the quality or condition of being whole or integrated – complete. Living with integrity is the best way to stay connected to your "inner wisdom." If you are not living with integrity, your goals become harder to reach, you attract the wrong people, and lose faith in yourself. Living with integrity means living up to the highest vision of you.

According to Don Miguel Ruiz (author of *The Four Agreements*), everything we do is based on agreements we have made: agreements with ourselves, other people, with God, and with life. But the most important agreements are the ones we make with ourselves. In these agreements we tell ourselves who we are, how to behave, what is possible, what is impossible. When we form agreements based upon fear, we deplete our energy, diminish our self-worth, and make living with integrity difficult, if not outright impossible.

Are you breaking promises to yourself? Are you out of touch with the person you really want to be? In fact, the simple recognition that you're out of touch – that you're not living your best life – can be a spiritual awakening for you. Consider this moment of self-discovery as reason to rejoice. Recommit yourself to a life of integrity. Here's how.

• Be impeccable with your word. Speak with integrity. Say only what you mean. Avoid using your word to speak ill of yourself (check your self-talk) or to gossip about others. Use the power of your word in the pursuit of truth and love.

• Don't take anything personally. What others say and do is a projection of their own reality, their own "stuff." When you are immune to the opinions and actions of others, you won't be the victim of needless suffering.

• Don't make assumptions. Find the courage to ask questions and to express what you really want. Communicate with others as clearly as you can to avoid misunderstandings, sadness, and drama. With just this one agreement, you can completely transform your life.

• Always do your best. Your best is going to change from moment to moment. It will be different when you are tired as opposed to well rested. Whatever the circumstance, simply do your best and you will avoid self-judgment, self-abuse, and regret.

These principles sound easy, even simplistic, but try keeping just one of them for an entire day. Living with integrity takes work, but in the process, you will become the person you say you are. Your words will reflect your actions; there will be no room in your life for lies – even small white ones. You will be living with integrity and living up to the highest vision of you.

Always Do Your Best

"When you do your best, you learn to accept yourself. But you have to be aware and learn from your mistakes. Learning from your mistakes means you practice, look honestly at the results, and keep practicing. This increases your awareness."

– Don Miguel Ruiz, *The Four Agreements*

When I was a kid in school and brought home news that I had fared poorly on a test, Mom would always ask me, "Did you do your best?" Sometimes, I could honestly answer yes; other times I would hang my head, kick the ground, and admit that I hadn't done my best.

I learned a valuable lesson one day when I brought home a school project and explained – exasperated – that I had done my best, worked my hardest, and yet received only a modest mark. Mom told me that my best effort was all anyone could ask of me.

She told me that I never had to feel bad, guilty, or disappointed if I had truly done my best.

"Always do your best," she said. "No more and no less."

Many years later, I had the pleasure of reading Don Miguel Ruiz' *The Four Agreements*. I was surprised and delighted to discover that Ruiz' fourth Toltec agreement was my mother's old maxim: always do your best.

Says Ruiz, "Everything is alive and changing all the time, so your best will sometimes be high quality, and other times it will not be as good. When you wake up refreshed and energized in the morning, your best will be better than when you are tired at night. Your best will be different when you are healthy as opposed to sick, or sober as opposed to drunk. Your best will depend on whether you are feeling wonderful and happy, or upset, angry, or jealous."

I was intrigued when Ruiz recommended we avoid trying to do more than our best. If we try too hard to force our performance, we may overdo it, deplete our body and go "against ourselves." It could even take us longer to accomplish our goals. Ruiz is not suggesting we cease striving to improve our performance. Always doing our best will result in consistent improvement. Despite our best efforts, the truth is we cannot deliver 110 percent. Our best is just that: 100 percent of our best effort at the time. When we always do our best, we are taking action. And by developing the attitude of always doing our best, we find ourselves doing it because we love it, not because we're expecting a reward. Most people do exactly the opposite: they only take action when they expect compensation, a reward, and often they don't enjoy the action.

In *The Four Agreements*, Ruiz cites the following example: "Most people go to work every day just thinking of payday and the money they will get from the work they are doing. They can hardly wait for Friday or Saturday, whatever day they receive their money and can take time off. They are working for the reward, and as a result, they resist work. They try to avoid the action and it becomes more difficult, and they don't do their best."

On the other hand, if you take action just for the love of doing it, without concern for compensation, you may find that you enjoy every action you do. Rewards will come, but you will not attach to them. And chances are the rewards will be more than just monetary.

When you do your best, you don't give your inner critic the chance to find you guilty. There are no regrets. You don't subject yourself to needless frustrations, self-judgment, and guilt. Always do your best. Toltec wisdom or simple motherly advice? Wise words either way.

Regular Maintenance

"All parts should go together without forcing. You must remember that the parts you are reassembling were disassembled by you. Therefore, if you can't get them together again, there must be a reason. By all means, do not use a hammer."

– IBM maintenance manual, 1925

"Here's the maintenance schedule for your new car," explained the sales rep, holding the small, blue book open before me. "I've already booked in your first regular maintenance appointment."

He went on to explain that the car company requires absolute adherence to the maintenance schedule. Apparently, many drivers in the past chose to ignore the program and (as a result) scores of vehicles went without regular oil changes and service work. "If you choose not to follow the schedule and later have a problem with the drive train, for example, the company will not honor your warranty."

I have always been a stickler for regular vehicle maintenance and found it fascinating that an auto manufacturer had to resort to such extreme measures to ensure something as simple as an oil change happened. The same lack of attention – regular maintenance – can damage a healthy relationship. I have found that little things, such as too little time and attention, will hurt an intimate relationship more than anything else will. We can usually get through the tough times, but it's neglect on a daily basis that often destroys closeness and intimacy.

In his book *The Romance Factor*, Alan Loy McGinnis says the longer we postpone maintenance, the faster the rate of deterioration. He writes, "I see that principle operating in families every day. Many couples who have come to my office with their marriages in shreds did not start fighting about unsolvable problems. Their marriages were not suffering from major malfunctions, but merely from a series of small deteriorations that a little adjusting and tightening could have corrected. But people had lost interest and had turned their attention to other things: careers, tennis, decorating their homes."

Everything of value requires time, attention and maintenance! In one week's time I worked on two plumbing problems at home, repaired a loose cupboard door, put trim around my new office door, wired a new light in the laundry room, and fixed the weather stripping around the back door. At the same time, our van needed two new tires, windshield wipers, and an oil change.

In another week I also took my son to a soccer game, volunteered for a project at work, helped my daughter with her English homework, called my mom, e-mailed my sister, shared a bottle of wine and stimulating conversation with my wife, and helped a good friend haul drywall and insulation into his home for a renovation project.

I'm in trouble if my home or automobile receive more attention than my closest relationships: family, work and friends. And like my home or vehicles, occasionally my relationships require a major service or repair and I must be up for the task. Truly, everything of value requires time, attention, and maintenance.

Stop for a moment and consider the last time you did some regular maintenance on your important relationships. I doubt anyone will be creating a relationship maintenance schedule anytime in the near future, but adhering to one could certainly prove worthwhile. Have you had a relationship fail because you didn't bother to do the maintenance?

Someone once told me, "Lack of regular maintenance will turn your valuable relationship from an *ideal* into an *ordeal*." Corny, but true. Daily maintenance – spending enough time, listening and touching, laughing and caring – will keep you close. And isn't that what we all long for?

Happiness and Self-Discipline

"Happiness makes up in height for what it lacks in length."

– Robert Frost, poet

In one of my columns on happiness, I wrote, "True happiness is a choice *you* have to make." At a recent workshop, one of the participants took exception to the statement.

"I *deserve* happiness!" she stated.

"Happiness a conscious choice," I replied.

"It's not a choice," she snapped. "I have a right to be happy!"

"Are you happy?" I questioned.

"No," she said, "but that doesn't mean I don't deserve to be!"

There is a tendency for some people to explain feelings of happiness or unhappiness in terms of the external events. They explain happiness by pointing to positive events, unhappiness by pointing to the negatives. The implication is that events determine whether we are happy or unhappy. I think our attitudes have far more to do with how happy we are than any external conditions.

Take a person who is primarily happy, meaning that he or she is happy a greater amount of the time than unhappy. Now, let some misfortune happen: the loss of a job or loved one, the breakup of a relationship, a disease, or physical disability. For a certain period, that individual will suffer because of the event. Then, check back in a few weeks, months, or even a year and (depending on the severity of the problem) the person will – most likely – be happy again.

In contrast, take a person who is primarily unhappy and let something wonderful happen – a promotion, winning the lottery, falling in love – and for a while he or she will be happy. However, check back and very likely you will find unhappiness again.

The best forecasters of our happiness are our self-esteem and the belief that we, rather than external forces, are the most significant shapers of our destiny.

My friend Diana (not her real name) is a true inspiration. I have never met anyone for whom joy is a more natural state. Yet her life has not always been easy. Growing up with an alcoholic father, Diana had more than her share of emotional abuse and heartache. Diana is happily married with two beautiful boys, is well on her way to becoming a successful children's author, and never speaks of past struggles with any hint of self-pity. I have seen her hit by disappointing experiences occasionally, seen her sad or subdued for a few hours (seldom more than a day), then watched her bounce back to her natural state of joy without any evidence of denial or repression. Her happiness is real and larger than any adversity.

When asked about her resiliency, Diana told me, "I choose to be happy." Then she added, "That takes self-discipline." She seldom closes her eyes at night without taking time to review everything good in her life – typically her last thoughts of the day. The more I spoke to and thought about happy people like Diana, the clearer it became to me that happy people process experiences in a different way. Positives are held in the foreground of consciousness and negatives are consigned to the background.

We can all learn a lesson from people like Diana. If you see someone who, in spite of life's adversities, is happy a good deal of the time, recognize that you are looking at a spiritual achievement and one worth aspiring to.

Happiness

"Remember that happiness is a way of travel – not a destination."

– Roy M. Goodman, State Senator from Manhattan's east side

Happiness. So many pursue it, yet so few seem able to capture and take hold of it. Is happiness truly elusive or do we simply not understand what it means to be happy? Perhaps happiness is not achieved by the conscious pursuit of it, but rather is the byproduct of other activities. With that thought in mind, here are some activities to consider.

Stop trying to control circumstances. One of the biggest "happiness busters" is the frustration people experience and wallow in because circumstances have gone amiss. The false belief is, "I should be able to control all circumstances." Let's set the record straight: you can't! Therefore, the first step toward happiness is to stop trying to control or take responsibility for circumstances that are simply beyond your control.

There's only one thing you *can* control in this world and that's you. You can't control the weather, other drivers, your kids, spouse, or anything for that matter outside of your own beliefs, thoughts, attitudes, and actions. When you relinquish your desire to control the external, you'll gain a much greater internal control.

Decide what you want out of life and stick with it. This is a two-part process. First, know what you want. Get clear with yourself. Take a private retreat to be alone if you have to, but come to grips with what you want your life to look like. Second, devote yourself to that passion and don't allow yourself to be sidetracked.

Be a day-maker, not a day-breaker. We can't be self-absorbed and live only for ourselves. Yes, we only control ourselves, but we can live for the betterment of others. Live life in such a way that others are touched by your good deeds, thoughts, and actions.

Settle your finances. Poor finances are a major cause of unhappiness. Some people are content with a modest income; others desire a little more. That's OK. We all have different desires, needs, and goals. But the key is to know what you want your financial life to look like and then do what it takes to get there. Among the major things to do is to eliminate debt. Get professional help if you need it. There are a number of excellent financial advisors out there who can help set you on the path to financial freedom.

Surround yourself with good friends. I am blessed with some of the most intelligent, capable, successful, and caring friends a person could have – people I admire and trust completely. Few things will bring more happiness into your life than a circle of good friends. Take time to develop your friendships. Spend time with friends – share, care, and do fun things with your friends. The busier your life becomes, the more you need the companionship and revitalizing power of friendship.

Develop your principal love relationship. Marriage will show you both heaven and hell. Marriage, when it's going well, will send you out the door each morning on Cloud Nine. When it isn't going well, it affects every area of your life. Work hard at developing your principal love relationship. The happiness you reap will be tremendous!

True happiness is a choice *you* have to make. It is a state of being only you can create. You don't find happiness; you make happiness by living a full and empowered life.

Don't Keep the Anger Inside

"Anybody can become angry, that is easy; but to be angry with the right person, and to the right degree, and at the right time, and for the right purpose, and in the right way, that is not within everybody's power and is not easy."

– Aristotle, ancient Greek philosopher

One of the first jobs I ever had was working on a neighbor's farm. Father thought it would be a good experience and a chance for me to see how other people did things. I would get off the school bus around four and spend a couple hours doing chores and helping.

New to farming, our neighbor was often frustrated by his lack of knowledge. I took to secretly calling him Chuck because each time he became angry, he would "chuck" whatever he was holding – a hammer, a wrench – once he threw his cap on the ground then stomped on it. Shortly after each outburst, he would feel a little sheepish and apologize.

"I just can't keep the anger inside," he'd say.

I'm reminded of a story about a woman who called her local police department to ask the penalty for fighting. The officer on duty told her the fine could be as high as $500. She might also be charged with assault and battery.

When he enquired as to why she was asking, she replied, "I want to punch my sister-in-law in the nose but I need to know if I can afford it first."

Anger must certainly be expressed, but there is a price for expressing it inappropriately. In the Japanese town of Yamanakako, visitors pay hefty sums for the chance to let their anger out. Yoshie Ogasawara's "Relief Room" is the main attraction of her four-storey fun house. There, stressed businesspersons, spurned lovers and furious spouses can smash a large porcelain vase, hurl ceramic ware into a soapstone peach tree and break a couple of ceramic clowns in order to discharge repressed rage. The phenomenal success of Yoshie's relief room is testament to our human need to express or release our anger.

Cultural factors come into play. Western culture places a high value on anger. We are supposed to feel moral outrage when someone steps on our rights and, in many conditions, we feel justified in trying to avenge or destroy people who wound us.

In Europe, the brave knight slays the dragon. In Asia, the hero speaks with the dragon, makes friends with the dragon, and uses its power to advance his cause.

We often use anger as an escape from other emotions that bother us even more. Anger feels strong, whereas our deeper feelings may be those of guilt, regret, or fear. It is easier to energize ourselves for a fight then accept self-responsibility for how we truly feel.

The simplest yet most effective way of dealing with anger is to express it in words. "Talk it out" with the person with whom you are upset. If it is not possible to talk directly with the offending party, find a good listener who is willing.

Write a letter to the person you are angry at but don't send it. After you are done, you can either tear the letter up or burn it safely, depending on how you feel.

Other suggestions might include cranking up the music and singing along while visualizing the anger flowing out of your body, punching a pillow, twisting a towel, walking or running on the trails – not to distract, but to help release your pent-up anger.

The anger must be expressed soon, since undeclared anger is like a malignant tumor. The Bible says, "Don't let the sun go down on your wrath." Strive to let go of each day's resentment in order to start the next day with a clean slate.

The late Mario Puzo, author of *The Godfather*, put it this way, "Never get angry. Never make a threat. Reason with people."

Talking is still the best way to work through life's issues. Besides, it saves you searching the grass for lost hammers and wrenches. It also keeps the dishes for company.

Discomfort in the Comfort Zone

"The comfort zone is seductive. We all desire comfort. It's human nature. However, too much comfort does not serve us well. An inability to step out of your comfort zone will profoundly limit your performance."

– Jim McCormick, motivational speaker and world champion skydiver

"Any news on the new job?" I asked my colleague. "It sounded pretty exciting."

"I blew off the interview," he admitted, and took a sip of his coffee. "Guess I'm just too comfortable where I'm at – it's not all bad."

A comfort zone happens when we settle too deeply into a routine. We stop doing all the things that make life and work fun, interesting, and challenging. We're not growing at the rate we once grew. In fact, we may not be growing at all, but stagnating – stuck in a rut. Research suggests one in four people work and live out their lives in an endless rut. I believe that number is low.

There is a difference between striving, with an occasional respite, and permanently dozing in the great parking lot of life. We can draw many comparisons here: striving versus surviving, pursuing versus responding, growing versus maintaining, and proacting versus reacting. The truth is there is only one way to coast: downhill.

Don't get me wrong; if you're tired and need a break to relax and rejuvenate, that's a good thing. When we are in pursuit mode for an extended length of time – striving, growing, and being proactive – we tire and need a rest.

Think back to a time when life was energizing and your work satisfying. Doubtless, you were learning, generating new ideas, trying to carve out a niche for yourself in the world – following your dreams. Your dreams in those days were big enough to make you giddy. You jumped out of bed in the morning without the assistance of an alarm clock. You may have had trouble falling asleep the night before because you were so excited about the next day. Pursuing your dream was more fun than fun. What happened?

Instead of thriving, you settled for surviving. You stopped reading, studying, and growing. You let the fun slip through your fingers. You fought the natural human urge to evolve.

Within each of us is the desire to grow, to improve, to evolve and to reach our full potential. Life itself is the ultimate journey toward self-actualization – the pinnacle in Maslow's *Hierarchy of Needs*: "to become everything that one is capable of becoming." All living creatures naturally strive to reach their full and complete expression. Among all living things, only humans make a conscious decision to stop growing.

None of us sets out to be mediocre. We just accept it somewhere along the path. Will you accept mediocrity? Will you shine like a bright light in the world? No one has a monopoly on potential; each of us carries our own around with us. Some of the world's most successful people believe that the roots of disappointment and guilt lie in our failure to pursue our potential.

When we begin again to dream of possibilities and look for new ways to solve old problems, when we fuel ourselves with knowledge that comes only from a commitment to life-long learning, then we begin to feel the blood coursing through our veins, letting us know that we are once again actively engaged in life. Only then, can we blast out of our comfort zones and reach new heights.

The Right to Be Wrong

"Take chances, make mistakes. That's how you grow. Pain nourishes your courage. You have to fail in order to practice being brave."

– Mary Tyler Moore, American actor

The exchange began over lunch and soon escalated. By the time my friend, Ceri and I had begun our walk back to work, the discussion had become a heated debate.

As we walked into the office, Ceri threw up her arms in frustration and announced, "That's it! End of discussion!" Determined to explain my point, I absentmindedly followed her through a doorway. Ignoring me, Ceri reached into her purse, pulled out a tube of lipstick, leaned toward the mirror, puckered up and began applying her "new mouth."

A couple women walked by and gasped, then hurriedly left the room. I looked up and saw my reflection in the large rectangular mirror above the sink. Ceri was smiling.

"What's so funny?" I asked.

"Do you often follow women into the washroom?"

Why do we often make our biggest mistakes in public? Some people can't avoid it. Former hockey goalie Jacques Plante once said, "How would you like a job where, if you made a mistake, a big red light goes on and 18,000 people boo?"

Embarrassment aside, we should never give up our right to be wrong. Good judgment comes from experience and experience comes from bad judgment. It is your right to be wrong occasionally.

"A life spent making mistakes is not only more honorable, but more useful than a life spent doing nothing," said George Bernard Shaw. Great mistakes are opportunities for great learning and great learning makes for great living.

I'm reminded of story that writer and motivator Steve Goodier shared about a newly appointed clergyman contacted by a local funeral director to hold a graveside service at a small country cemetery. There was to be no funeral, just the committal, because the deceased had no family or friends left in the state.

The young pastor started out early for the cemetery, but soon became lost. After making several wrong turns, he finally arrived a half-hour late. The hearse was nowhere in sight and cemetery workers were relaxing under a nearby tree, eating their lunch.

The pastor went to the open grave and found that the vault lid was already in place. He took out his book and read the service. As he returned to his car, he overheard one of the workers say, "Maybe we'd better tell him it's a septic tank."

You have the right to be wrong. If you want to build a great life, you have a duty to make great mistakes – it's how we learn. If you can, laugh at your mistakes. Always learn from them and try to make sure your next mistake is one you haven't made before!

There is a lesson in every mistake. Successful people prosper in life because of a tendency to cut their losses, thereby minimizing mistakes. It is only when people refuse to accept that they have made a bad choice or decision and move from acceptance into resistance that a mistake becomes potentially devastating.

When you accept your mistakes, you can deal with circumstances as facts and realities, rather than hoping, wishing and praying that it would or could be different. Once you stop resisting "what is" you can begin to make wise and informed decisions. It's the first step in becoming a far more positive, creative and constructive person.

Freedom

"You can't separate peace from freedom because no one can be at peace unless he has his freedom."

– Malcolm X, human rights activist

In his best selling book, *The Five Secrets*, writer and corporate motivator Pat Lynch tells the story of a group of kids and adults who were asked, "If you were an animal, would you rather live free in the wild where it's dangerous and you have to find your own food and water, or would you rather live in the zoo, behind bars? The zoo staff will take good care of you, give you food and water, and every day people will come and stare at you?" The kids chose to live free in the wild, but most of the adults chose the zoo and came up with countless good reasons why they had no other option.

Each week I have the pleasure of spending a few minutes chatting with Frank Pavlick, Canada's Sports Poet, and each time Frank gives me a new insight to consider or a challenge to accept. This past week he told me he'd concluded – after 60 years of living – that the most important word in our vocabulary is "freedom."

"Freedom?" I queried. "Not peace, love, or integrity?"

"Freedom," declared Frank. "Think about it and you'll know I'm right!"

When I returned to my desk, I typed "freedom" onto the blank page and clicked the definitions button. "Noun: The condition of being free; the power to act, speak, or think without externally imposed restraints." I considered the definition and then had an insight. Immediately, I changed "externally" to "internally" imposed restraints.

How many of us have traded our freedom for what we perceive as security? Most of us have been programmed from childhood to believe that someone else has our answers or knows what's best for us. By relinquishing our self-responsibility, we climb into the cage and become a passive observer rather than an active participant in our life. Because of our programming, taking control feels so strange, uncomfortable, and inappropriate that most of us choose not to do it. Not because we can't, but because we won't. Rather than take control and run our own lives, most of us choose to give up. To settle. To take the path of least resistance and surrender our dreams and freedom.

If you're ever to be truly free, you must reclaim control and make it happen, because it's all up to you! Start today by refusing to spend the rest of your days whining (Why does this always happen to me?) and take back your power – the power you've had all along. Choose to live by eight simple little words: "If it's to be, it's up to me!" No more excuses, complaining, or pretending you're the "helpless victim" of life. Are you willing to be the master of your own destiny? If you make that choice, you're saying you're tired of not getting what you want, just taking and making excuses. You're also through putting up with people who spend their lives whining and complaining – including yourself. Does the idea frighten you? Good. Then it's worthy of your full effort.

Beginning right away, quit arguing for your limitations and waiting for the "right conditions" to show up before acting. If the conditions are not there when you need them, create them! Believe in yourself, accept your power, and let yourself have what you've always wanted. And refuse to give up until you get it! Do it: make the choice and reclaim your dreams and your freedom. Thanks Frank.

Be a Good One

My mother said to me, "If you become a soldier, you'll be a general; if you become a monk, you'll end up as Pope." Instead, I became a painter and wound up as Picasso.

– Pablo Picasso, Spanish painter and sculptor

In the community where I grew up, we had a bachelor named Bob who did a little farming, but primarily made his living repairing tractor and implement tires. Bob had a quirky sense of humor and a wheezy, contagious laugh that always started me giggling. And no matter when you called Bob, he always seemed to arrive just before mealtime. Being a bachelor, Bob enjoyed a good home-cooked meal and always welcomed the offer of a second helping with, "Don't mind if I do!"

Bob was a simple man. He had little formal schooling. It seemed to me that Bob required little to be happy: a little work, a good meal from time to time, and the friendship of neighbors who appreciated his help.

One day Bob came rattling into our yard, the box of his old pickup filled with railway ties, hydraulic jacks, pry bars, and assorted tools. I stood with father, watching as Bob leaned against the huge back tractor tire, cautiously pumping out the caustic calcium chloride used for weight. I marveled at how Bob knew exactly where to position each jack and every railway tie – ensuring the tractor remained stable during the repair.

I looked up at father. "Bob sure is a good tire repair man."

"Whatever you are," replied father, "it's best to be a good one."

I think it helps to remember that excellence is not a place at which we arrive so much as a way of traveling. A journey rather than a destination.

In his inspirational book, *Deciding How to Live*, Steve Goodier tells the story of Viennese-born composer Frederick Loewe.

We remember Loewe from his musical scores that include *My Fair Lady, Gigi* and *Camelot.*

Loewe was not always famous. He studied piano with the great masters of Europe and achieved huge success as a musician and composer in his early years. But when he immigrated to the United States, he failed as a piano virtuoso.

For a while, he tried other types of work including prospecting for gold and boxing. But he never gave up his dream and continued to play piano and write music.

During those lean years, he could not always afford to make payments on his piano. One day, bent over the keyboard, he heard nothing but the music that he played with such rare inspiration. When he finished and looked up, he was startled to find that he had an audience – three moving men who were seated on the floor.

They said nothing and made no movement toward the piano. Instead, they dug into their pockets, pooled together enough money for the payment, placed it on the piano and walked out, empty-handed. Moved by the beauty of his music, these men recognized excellence and responded to it.

Perhaps, like Frederick Loewe, what you choose to be good at will inspire others and change the world or maybe, like Bob, your good skills will help neighbors and garner for you their respect and friendship – maybe a home-cooked meal, occasionally.

What's important is this: whatever you are, be a good one. If what you do is worth doing, if you believe that you are a valuable person, then you can't afford to be content with mediocrity. When you choose the path of excellence through this life, you will bring to it your best and receive the best it can offer in return.

Factor Number Three Summary: Self-Responsibility

To perform at your best and to feel terrific about yourself, you have to be in a perpetual state of building self-esteem and maintaining it – pushing yourself beyond your usual mental and emotional limits. You need to take complete responsibility for the content and quality of your mind and the attainment of your dreams.

Here are some questions and statements pertaining to self-responsibility that you may wish to ponder by yourself or discuss as a group.

1. When I feel I am being treated unfairly, I stand up and express my view honestly.
2. I care enough to confront inequities in my life and the lives of others in need.
3. I openly accept responsibility for my words and actions and – when necessary – make amends and apologize.
4. I make a conscious effort to remain in the moment and seldom look back on the past with regret or project fearfully into the future.
5. I speak with integrity and avoid using statements that lack self-responsibility.
6. I understand that I am the architect of my own destiny – I alone am responsible for building and maintaining my level of self-esteem and self-worth.
7. I am able to evaluate the insights and opinions of others without taking it personally or having differing views negatively affect my self-esteem.
8. I recognize how old values, beliefs, and perceptions filtered my life experience and I choose now to consciously remove those filters and see the world with fresh eyes.

"The first step toward mastering your destiny is simply acknowledging that it's possible to exert control over your life. Some people believe it, yet few rise to the challenge. For many, destiny is a curious, even mystical concept. For some, destiny means life is controlled – even predestined – by external forces over which we have little or no control."

– Murray Fuhrer, *Extreme Esteem*

Factor Number Four:
Effecting Change

The Maker gathered together all of creation and he said, "I want to hide something from mankind until he is ready to receive it. It is the realization that man is the architect of his own destiny."

The eagle said, "Give it to me, I will take it to the highest mountain top."

"No," the Maker said, "One day man will climb there and find it."

The salmon said, "Let me take it on the bottom of the deepest river."

"No," came the reply. "Man will venture there someday, too."

The buffalo suggested, "I can lose it on the Great Plains."

The Maker shook his head. "Man will cross the Great Plains and happen upon it."

Then from amid the crowd stepped tiny, nearly blind Grandmother Mole. "Man seldom looks inside himself for answers," she said. "Hide it deep inside his heart."

The crowd fell silent.

After a long wait, the Maker smiled and said, "So be it."

As humans, we're often engaged in a search for what we believe is missing in our lives: love, peace, opportunity, prosperity, good self-esteem, the ideal partner, the perfect job. We believe that if we find what is missing, then we will be complete and happy. The paradox is that often the answers we search for are both within us and in front of us.

You can surrender your destiny to the desires of others or you can shape your destiny by becoming an active, responsible participant in your own life. You have the choice.

The first step toward mastering your destiny is simply acknowledging that it's possible to exert control over your life. Some people believe it, yet few rise to the challenge. For many, destiny is a curious, even mystical concept. For some, destiny means life is controlled – even predestined – by external forces over which we have little or no control.

The obvious problem with such notions of life is that they relieve us of responsibility for our actions and rob us of incentive to live up to our potential. I call it the "conveyor belt" mentality: step onto the belt, close your eyes, and drop off dead at the end. Only when we step back and take an honest look at our life can we begin to see how our actions and choices have helped shape the course of our lives. To progress, succeed, and reap the rewards of our efforts, each of us must chart his own course through life.

Should you choose to become the architect, consider the following questions. Where do your talents lie and are they being used to the fullest in your current profession? Have you set realistic goals for yourself and tracked their progress? Have you nurtured positive affiliations to help you succeed? Have you accepted full responsibility for past choices? Will you face the consequences of choices you make today and in the future?

Shakespeare once wrote, "It is not in the stars to hold our destiny but in ourselves." You can look at your life in two ways: that your destiny is something that happens to you, or that it's something you actively create. For me, the choice here is obvious. Become the architect of your own life. We each have the power, through our own actions, to create a more rewarding destiny for ourselves. Be the one who makes things happen!

Building a Fence

"Your self-esteem is probably the most important part of your personality. It is the energy source or the reactor core of your personality. People with high self-esteem are more positive, more likable and more effective in every part of their lives."

– Brian Tracy, international writer, speaker, motivator

One summer, during my 17th year, I built a quarter mile of fence by hand: staking a long length of twine, starting each hole with a crowbar, pounding posts with a 13-pound post maul, cutting planks by hand, and hammering each board securely in place.

It was hard work, but I loved every minute of it. I loved the way my muscles felt when I pushed myself beyond my usual physical limits. I loved the crack of the maul as each strike drove the treated posts deeper and deeper into the hard ground. Most of all, I loved the sense of accomplishment I felt when I hammered the final spike into place. The fence was real – tangible – and each time I looked at it, I felt empowered. The fence took me a week to complete and each afternoon my mother would bring me lunch, admire my workmanship and encourage me to keep going.

When the fence was completed, both my parents came out to have a look. Mom stood by me as Father heaved on a couple posts. They were unyielding. He walked to the end of the run and eyeballed it. Father was not prone to compliments, so when he said, "That's a good true fence, son," I was thrilled. The feeling was intoxicating. I have seldom felt more proud.

Building your self-esteem is like building a fence. Swinging the maul helped raise my level of physical fitness. Your level of self-esteem is really your level of "mental fitness." It is a measure of how healthy, hardy, and resilient you are in dealing with life. To perform at your best and to feel terrific about yourself, you have to be in a perpetual state of building self-esteem and maintaining it – pushing yourself beyond your usual mental and emotional limits. Just as you take responsibility for your level of physical fitness, you need to take complete responsibility for the content and quality of your mind.

As with building the fence, self-esteem is a condition you experience when moving systematically toward the accomplishment of something important to you. For that reason, it is vital to have clear goals for each part of your life and to work continually toward achieving those goals. Each progressive step causes your self-esteem to go up and makes you feel more positive and effective in everything else you do.

Building self-esteem involves having success experiences. Once you set your goals, it is important to make them measurable so you can track small and large achievements. Each day I would set a goal for my fence and each evening I would look back on the work accomplished and plan for the next day. The very act of setting up a goal, breaking it down into smaller parts, and then completing those parts makes you feel like a success.

A vital component of building self-esteem is recognition of your accomplishments by people whom you respect. Whenever you are recognized and praised for any accomplishment by someone whose opinion you hold in high regard, your self-esteem goes up, along with your eagerness and enthusiasm to do even better on the job next time.

Part of the old fence is still standing on the family farm and even today, I can lean against a top plank, feel those solid old posts, and re-experience a wonderful sense of accomplishment. Start building your new fence today and enjoy the journey!

The Value of the Hour

"If you want to be truly successful, invest in yourself."

– Sidney Madwed, writer, speaker, motivator

Years ago, someone asked me if I could appreciate the value of an hour. I can't recall my response, but I do recall the words told to me. An hour was priceless. "Devote one hour each day to pursuing your dreams," I was told, "and you'll change the world." Years later, I read that one hour each day adds up to nine 40-hour weeks over the course of a year.

As you can imagine, I was blown away when I had it put to me that way. Nine 40-hour weeks? This seemed impossible until I did the math: 365 days, times one hour each is nine 40-hour weeks! Think about it. How good could you become at something if you did it all day, every day for just over two months? I think you already know the answer.

Imagine as well, how good you could become at some things if you did them for just one hour a day for the next year. How much fitter would you get? How much more love and devotion could you share with your family? How much more money could you earn? If you invested one hour a day in your personal development, in the attainment of your goals, over five years you would have invested the equivalent of 1,825 hours.

One hour is a small price to pay in comparison to the payoff. Just one hour a day may be the investment you need to get the results you want and desire from your life. Is getting what you want worth an hour a day? I certainly think so.

For me, the decision was simple. I have been studying self-esteem and empowerment for nearly a decade now. Each time I think I have a solid grip on the concept, the universe gently reminds me of how little I know and how much more there is to learn and observe.

You must decide which hour works best for you. In our busy world, an hour can seem elusive – almost beyond our grasp.

Family and work obligations, over-commitment and even out-and-out fatigue can make the idea of setting an hour aside for ourselves seem just about unmanageable. If you can't set aside a full hour in one block, take two half-hour breaks to work on you and your dreams. The hour shouldn't be drudgery either, but a time you look forward to enjoying. I manage to set aside my hour to read motivational books – usually just before retiring for the evening. I also carry motivational CDs in my car to listen to as I drive to and from work. They are the fuel for my mind and it keeps me learning and yearning for more. Find time where and when you can – start planning for it today.

Can you appreciate the value of an hour? An hour is priceless. A wise person once said, "You can't take out of life more than you put in." Please agree to set aside one hour a day for yourself. Choose one area of your life that you want to improve and commit the next 90 days to that one thing. The results you achieve will be well worth the investment! And you know, it really is true: devote one hour each day to pursuing your dreams and you'll change the world.

Being in the Now

"Usually, the future is a replica of the past. Superficial changes are possible, but real transformation is rare and depends upon whether you can become present enough to dissolve the past by accessing the power of the Now."

– Eckhart Tolle, adapted from *The Power of Now*

Sad fact: we often are so caught up in looking ahead or behind we forget to enjoy the moment – the now. We say things such as "I will be happy/secure/satisfied when … (you choose the words)." Sometimes we look behind and feel regret for what we did or didn't do – what did or didn't happen. Other times we peer expectantly into the future – convinced the keys to our personal happiness and success await us somewhere in that distant realm.

The first step toward moving into the now is to assess where you spend the majority of your time. Step back and consider your everyday emotional state. Are you constantly filled with regret, shame, or guilt? Your mind is dwelling in the past. Are you overwhelmed by fear, anxiety, or apprehension? Your thoughts are focused on the future.

The now is all we have. We cannot change the past and the only way to influence the future is by our actions in the now. Focus on the now and understand you are the only one who determines your reality. Decide what it is you will and won't do with your time, what you will and won't think, what actions you will undertake right now. The most powerful force in the universe is a focused mind. Put all the energy you previously focused on your past or future and apply it to the now – to this moment.

When you begin to watch your mind, you will soon discover that it's a noisy place, filled with endless thoughts and images. Research suggests as many as 60,000 thoughts flash through your mind each day. Watch those thoughts, and you'll discover how each is connected to events from the past or to what you think will or should happen in the future. An unfocused mind is a weary mind – fluctuating between anger arising from frustrated expectations and worries concerning the future.

If we train ourselves to watch our thoughts, mindfully, without being swayed by emotion, we become the witness rather than the unwitting participant. We discover that our thoughts are loaded with values and judgments about what we have come to believe is good and what is not good and how we believe things should be in the world.

A simple exercise to remain in the now is being aware of every time you escape from the present by fantasizing about the past or future. When you find yourself drifting into the past or projecting into the future immediately focus your attention on your breathing. This will anchor you in the moment. Sit comfortably, close your eyes, and inhale slowly. Feel the sensation under your nose and follow the inhalation. Then exhale slowly. Follow the breath, feel the sensation, and then inhale again. Be mindful of the breathing and the sensations. Be aware of when the air is going in and when the air is going out.

Staying in the present can return us to center and balance and provide us with the power and focus we need to set realistic goals and achieve our greatest dreams. The now is the domain of the passionate learner – the lifelong student. It opens the mind to endless possibilities, providing understanding, and meaning in each moment of our lives.

A Thousand Marbles

"How old would you be if you didn't know how old you were?

– Satchel Paige, Baseball Hall of Fame inductee

Norm Williams was 67 years old when I met him back in 1986, but I would have guessed him to be a decade younger. After retiring from his career as a television writer, Norm took a sales job at a small radio station in Kelowna, B.C. Tall and lanky, Norm moved briskly through his day with an easy stride and his hand was quick to be outstretched, ready to shake yours with enthusiasm.

When it came time for action, Norm would snap his fingers, pound his fist into his palm and say, “Today won’t last forever, so let’s make the most of it!”

By his example, Norm taught me that age is an idea – that growing old is a choice.

When I think about age and the passage of time, I’m reminded of the story *A Thousand Marbles* by author and motivator, Jeffrey Davis. The story tells of an older man, a guest on a radio talk show, and the conversation he has with a caller named Tom.

“Let me tell you something Tom,” says the older man. “Something that has helped me keep a good perspective on my own priorities.

“The average person lives about 75 years. I know, some live more and some live less, but on average folks live about 75 years.

“If you sit down and do a little arithmetic, you’ll discover that 75 times 52 equals 3,900 – which is the number of Saturdays that the average person has in their entire lifetime.

“It took me until I was 55 years old to think about all this in any detail and by that time, I had lived through over 2,800 Saturdays. I got to thinking that if I lived to be 75, I only had about a thousand of them left to enjoy.

“So I went to a toy store and bought every single marble they had. I ended up having to visit three toy stores to round up 1,000 marbles. I took them home and put them inside of a large, clear plastic container right here in my workshop next to the radio. Every Saturday since then I have taken one marble out and have thrown it away.

“I found that by watching the marbles diminish, I focused more on the important things in life. There is nothing like watching your time here on this earth run out to help get your priorities straight.

"This morning, I took the last marble out of the container. I figure if I make it until next Saturday then God has blessed me with a little extra time to be with my loved ones."

Want to stay young? Here's what I've learned from people like Norm.

Eat well, exercise often, respect and care for your body.

Toss out unneeded numbers including age, weight and height.

Keep only cheerful friends. The grouches pull you down.

Keep learning. Never let your brain be idle.

Enjoy the simple things. Spend some time watching the sunrise.

Laugh often, long and loud. Laugh until you gasp for breath.

Tears happen. Endure, grieve, and move on. We are the only person with us for the entire journey.

Be an example to others. You will be either a good example or an example of what not to be. Choose to be a good example.

Finally and perhaps most importantly, be alive while you're still living. Someone once told me, "Work like you don't need the money. Love as if you've never been hurt. Dance as if no one's watching."

Adolf's Tennis Court

"We must not allow the clock and the calendar to blind us to the fact that each moment of life is a miracle and mystery."

– H. G. Wells, English novelist, journalist, sociologist, and historian

It was a good house – a practical house – and Adolf stood before it, admiring the workmanship. Adolf and his wife, Elsie had eight children. The family had needed a new house for some time and this fine home was perfect with its spacious kitchen, comfortable living room, four large bedrooms, full basement, and (finally) an indoor bathroom.

"Elsie has her big kitchen," said Adolf with pride. "Now she can cook even better!"

Adolf's new job with Alberta Agriculture meant the family could finally relax the purse strings and start enjoying life. For over 20 years, Adolf had scratched a living from the land. The new job meant time away from the family for Adolf, a burden for Elsie, but the couple believed the sacrifices worthwhile.

Now, in fall of 1965, Adolf stood with my father (his close friend) discussing the future. Father eyed a large rectangle of black earth on the east side of the new house.

"That's going to make a fine garden plot," said Father.

"Oh no," laughed Adolf. "No garden plot – that's for my tennis court."

"Tennis court?" asked Father. "Where did you get such a notion?"

"One time," Adolf confided, "when I was in the city, I stopped to watch some people playing tennis." He paused.

"Have you ever watched tennis, Albert?" Father shook his head. "Well, it's quite the game. They say that when you play it, you don't think about yesterday or tomorrow; all you think about is the game. It's all there is. I want to know that feeling."

Adolf never found the leisure or the funds to build his tennis court. The rectangle of earth became a fine garden plot and a sanctuary when Elsie passed away.

Years later, two old friends sat at a kitchen table sharing coffee and a reminiscence or two. Gradually, the conversation wound its way along a familiar country road and back to a distant tennis court. Adolf grew quiet and sat staring out the kitchen window.

"You know that feeling?" he said. "No yesterday or tomorrow – only the game?"

Father nodded.

"I've felt that way. Playing with the kids when they were little and now playing with the grandkids. Sometimes, I'd feel it at work. I feel it often now when I'm in the garden. Looking back, I guess I felt it the most when Elsie and I would just sit and talk."

How many times have you said, "Time goes so fast?" Moments come and go as we do our "important" tasks of the day. Our focus seems to be on what needs to be done instead of on what we can do with the moments we are given. Quantity becomes more important than quality and precious moments disappear one by one into the shadows of our life.

Renowned author, Henry Miller put it this way, "Every moment is a golden one for he who has the vision to recognize it as such."

In the midst of your frantic day, stop and be thankful for this time here on earth. Celebrate the fact you're alive and see the wonder contained within each moment.

Seize the moments of your life and allow each to create magic. See each as a miracle and know that within each lies the secret of happiness. Live in the present and make it so beautiful it will be worth remembering. This alone will change your world.

Mindfulness

"If past to future is on a horizontal line, then the present moment is not in time, but a vertical movement transcending time."

– Osho, author and teacher of *Enlightenment*

Mindfulness – I'm hearing the word increasingly in self-esteem and empowerment circles. Mindfulness is often used in the sense of "living in the moment." When being mindful, you are not judging, reflecting, or thinking. You are simply observing the moment in which you find yourself. Mindfulness is not an attempt to make the moment pleasant or pain-free (though that might be a side benefit). The moment may be enjoyable, arousing, empty, awkward, upsetting, or stressful, but it is – in its most basic form – an experience. We suffer as the result of labeling that experience or by judging it.

Much of the time, our experience lacks a quality of awareness or mindfulness. Often, we travel through life on cruise control, automatically living out habitual patterns of behavior. Without awareness, habitual tendencies can take over and run our lives. As we begin to develop our personal level of mindfulness, it can be shocking to discover just how habitual our lives have become and how runaway thinking has led to our suffering. When we're on cruise control, we're not mindfully aware of what's going on. We may know on some level that we're troubled but never investigate those feelings fully or acknowledge our responsibility for resolving them. We fantasize without any discernment of whether what we're thinking about is making us happy or distressed.

When we are not being mindful in the moment, we often lose ourselves – brooding about some past hurt or fantasizing about a future in which we have won the lottery, are living in paradise, or matched with the perfect loving partner. Seldom are these fantasized pasts and futures reality-based, but rather imaginings of how things might be, could be, or ought to be in our reckoning. And as with all unmindful activity, we have no awareness that this fantasizing is pointless. All it does is add force to disruptive emotional tendencies that can never truly enrich our lives.

There are, of course, ways of mindfully thinking about the past or future. We can reflect on the past and think about how our experience has provided us with knowledge, insights, and wisdom that we can put into positive practice in the now. We can think about the future, but rather than it being idle daydreaming, we think about the consequences of our actions today and reflect on where we want to be tomorrow. When we think about the past or future while being in the moment – while being mindful – we are conscious of our reflecting or projecting and never lost in thought. We don't confuse fantasy with reality. We don't stray from the moment, but instead bring to bear the full force of our knowledge and wisdom in the moment to create actively a future filled with power, intention, and focus. Our thinking is grounded, well considered, and purposeful. Think about it: the only way to change the past is to change the now, the moment.

Being mindful takes practice. As a wise Zen master said, "Stop seeking the truth; seek [instead] to let go of your opinions." Or, as Sergeant Joe Friday said on the *Dragnet* TV series, "Just the facts, ma'am." We only get to live our lives moment by moment; either we are here for them, or we're not. If we're not, life will simply slip away.

Dare to Dream Again

"Far better it is to dare mighty things, to win glorious triumphs, even though checkered by failure, than to take rank with those poor spirits who neither enjoy nor suffer much, because they live in the gray twilight that knows neither victory nor defeat."

– Teddy Roosevelt

Do you remember when you were a child and no dream seemed too big? When we were young, we shared a common trait: we were dreamers. Eventually, most of us started to let our dreams die. People began to tell us that we couldn't do the things we wanted to. It was impossible. Responsible people don't pursue their dreams. Settle down, get a job, and be dependable. Take care of business, live the mundane, be content.

Believe me, it's time to dream again and here are just a few reasons.

Avoiding regret. Someday we will all lie on our deathbed looking back through the history of our lives. Will you say, "Job well done," or will you regret the decisions you made and the opportunities you missed? I don't want to regret what could have been or what should have been and neither should you. Choose today to say, "I have decided today to pursue my dreams."

Making the world a better place. All of the great accomplishments began with a person who had a dream. Somebody rebuffed the naysayer and said, "This can be done and I am just the person to do it." I'm not speaking strictly of the larger-than-life variety of dreams. Think of all the people who volunteer their time, talents, and energy daily with the dream of making their neighborhoods and communities a better place. The world needs people like you to dream of something great and then to pursue it. Maybe you work for a business, school, or organization that started out with good intentions but has settled into the same old same old. Shake up the people around you – remind them of those good intentions and how they could make a difference again if they would only dream!

Personal and family fulfillment. A little piece of us dies when we stop pursuing our dreams. Stepping up and pursuing our dream rekindles that passion and lets us experience fulfillment. Having a purpose puts pride in our stride and power in our passions!

Leaving a legacy. How will your children remember you? Our children need to see that we dream; that we search for something better. They in turn will do the same!

So where do you start? Here are some ideas.

Reconnect with your dream. Set aside some time to let yourself dream. What have you placed on the back burner in order to live the status quo? Settle on one or two dreams that you can and will pursue. Don't come up with too many. That will only divide your energies.

Decide to do it. This may seem elementary but many people never decide and commit fully to their dream. They simply keep "thinking" about it.

Develop a systematic plan. This is essential. You must sit down and write out a few things such as a timeline. How long will it take to accomplish? What are the action steps? Point by point, what will you do and when will you do it?

List resources you will need to draw from. What will it take? Who will need to be involved for help or advice?

Create an evaluation tool. You need to evaluate from time to time whether or not you're making progress.

Plan a celebration. Celebrate your accomplishment once you've succeeded. Make it big! Reaching your dreams is worth celebrating.

There is no better time than now. Set aside some time today to get started on your dream. Become like the child again and reclaim your dreams and your destiny!

Entertain a Thought

"It is the mark of an educated mind to be able to entertain a thought without accepting it."

– Aristotle, ancient Greek philosopher

What separated great thinkers like Leonardo da Vinci from his contemporaries? Writer and motivational speaker, Maya Talisman Frost claims to know the answer. "They learned to entertain a thought." Maya claims it's remarkably simple and suggests that everyone learn to be a good host to new ideas and treat each new idea like a guest.

Let's say you see a quotation in a magazine, on a bus bench, or as Maya suggests, "on the side of a bus somewhere," and it "twigs" something inside. As you move through the day, you find yourself "bumping" into the new idea. It begins to move up the rankings in your mind until it has your full awareness. You decide to explore the concept further.

First, you'll need to clear some of the clutter in your mind to make room for the new idea. According to Deepak Chopra, the average human has 60,000 thoughts a day. Of those, 57,000 are the same ones you had yesterday! That's some serious clutter! Get rid of a few of those dusty old thoughts and make room for new ones.

Just like a guest in your home, a new idea will be more readily accepted if you actively and purposely introduce it to other ideas and interests. Look for unusual or inspired pairings. How *does it fit?* Where does it fit? *Does it fit*? You won't know until you try. Picture Leonardo da Vinci mentally entertaining his new idea – human flight. Immediately, Leonardo sets about to introduce his new idea to the other guests. To quote Talisman Frost, "Human Flight, meet my good friend, Engineering, and his lovely wife, Fabric Design. Oh, and have you met Bird Anatomy? She lives just around the corner from you. Now, you all make yourselves comfy and I'll go get some more wine."

So, what happened at Leo's party? He introduced his new idea to his existing thoughts and knowledge. What emerged was the idea for a perfectly designed parachute as well as a remarkable helicopter – hundreds of years before the Wright brothers and Kitty Hawk. Every time you entertain a new thought, your brain creates a new neural pathway. Introducing it to other thoughts creates a stronger, deeper, and clearer mental connection.

Listen, inquire, and show interest. Ask questions. Dig a little deeper. Find the connections to other people, places, and activities. Learn as much as you can about your new idea. Relinquish control. Don't direct the flow of ideas. Just let things happen. Leave room for future possibilities. You're not going to like every idea that comes your way. And you might not find any other interest or idea that connects with it initially. That's fine. You need to develop the ability to recognize useful concepts and distinguish valuable and valid ideas from those lacking a strong foundation. That's what critical thinking is all about. But you also need to file that idea away so that you can look it up when you *do* encounter a likely candidate for another gathering of your thoughts.

Entertain in whatever style suits you. It doesn't matter, as long as it's happening. Learn how to entertain a thought. With a little effort, you'll become the perfect host to new ideas. And guess what? You'll have no cleaning up to do the next morning.

A Positive Attitude

"There is nothing you cannot be. Nothing you cannot do. There is nothing you cannot have! Once you learn the simple principles of mastering a positive attitude, all that you want you will have."

– Joe Fermano, founder of The Positive Attitude Institute

I awaken each morning expecting the best. Give that statement some thought and you'll gain some insight into your personality. Do you view the world in a positive or negative way? A positive person will see the good in what may be a difficult situation and not give up when times get tough. Being positive means you believe in yourself, expect to do well, and believe that things can and will get better. Having a positive attitude is a good way to cope with stresses and problems of any size or nature.

Negative people tend to expect the worst things to happen and see nothing but black at the end of the tunnel. They view problems in a negative light and often think there's no use trying because things simply wouldn't work out anyway. A negative attitude is damaging to our self-esteem, leaving us doubtful, restricted, feeling hopeless, sad, and unwilling to try new experiences or meet new people. The best thing about a positive attitude is that it keeps us going and gives us hope. It's like seeing the light at the end of the tunnel and carrying a bright torch to guide you toward it.

No one can make you become positive; only you can make that choice. If you're finding it difficult to believe in yourself or to expect the best from each day, here are a few techniques that may help. Talk to someone you love, or who you think might have been in a similar situation, for advice and reassurance. On a piece of paper, make a scale from one to 10 (one being the worst thing you could imagine happening to you and 10 being the best) and then rate on this scale what's happening currently. Writing things down or talking aloud can help you check your attitude and self-talk.

Affirmations are another technique to develop a positive attitude. Create a short positive statement about yourself and a goal you will achieve in the future. Write it in the present tense and proclaim it as though it's already part of your reality. "Each day and in every way I'm growing more and more confident!" Repeat your affirmation at least once a day – believe it and believe in yourself! As well, spending some time with people who can see the bright or funny side of life can encourage you to have a more positive outlook and make you laugh.

Positive people understand that life isn't always perfect. You can't force yourself to smile or think positively and feel happy about every single situation – that's just not realistic. Life is a bit like a game of snakes and ladders – sometimes you go up and up only to slide back down again on your next turn. What you can do is believe that you can get straight up the top again with another roll of the dice.

A positive attitude or outlook on life can lead to positive behavior and create success. An upbeat, positive person draws other people like a magnet. After all, whom would you rather be around – someone who is strong and motivated with the confidence to keep moving forward or someone who stays stuck in one place, thinking of reasons why things don't seem to happen or won't work out for them? No contest!

Optimism

"Few things in the world are more powerful than a positive push. A smile. A word of optimism and hope. A 'You can do it' when things are tough."

– Richard M. DeVos, co-founder and former president, Amway Corporation

Optimism is a vital ingredient for a life that is creative, productive, and enjoyable. Optimism can be defined as the ability to expect the best outcome from any circumstance. Studies have proven that optimism is vital to success in both personal and business relationships. People who approach tasks in a positive manner and can recover quickly from adversity are the ones who ultimately succeed. Optimists are more resilient and persistent, less inhibited, more open to new ideas, and quicker to comprehend new concepts.

For some, optimism comes naturally. For most, it is an attitude towards life that must be learned and cultivated. The good news is that optimism and pessimism are learned behaviors. According to the latest research, optimists and pessimists are made, not born.

When we are optimistic, we find the "lesson" in everything that happens to us – whether good or unfortunate. When something good happens, we are grateful and take note of whatever we've been doing to provide the good results. We incorporate these actions and attitudes in the next situation and then give thanks for our ongoing success. If something unfortunate happens, we ask as well what lessons we need to learn from the experience. What are we doing that has given us an unfortunate result? What do we need to do next time to prevent such an outcome? The optimistic person puts a plan in place so the unproductive behaviors that result in undesirable situations don't repeat.

If the result we're hoping for falls somewhere in between – neither good nor bad, but simply average – we can make a note to consciously identify our inadequacies and determine what needs to be done to create a more positive outcome next time around.

So, if an optimistic attitude can be learned and cultivated, how and where do we start?

• Start by saying please and thank you to your higher power, your God, and to the positive people in your life. Tell them what they did or said that made a difference and why.

• Give one compliment, one supportive statement, or an encouraging word to at least one person each day.

• Work hard not to say "no," "won't," "can't," "never," or "that's not my job." These are "go nowhere" statements and can quickly label you as having a bad/negative attitude.

• Limit your time with negative, blaming, or whining people. They have the potential to drain you of your energy, your enthusiasm, and your optimism! Make an effort to resolve negativity with another person. If it can't be done or you don't see hope in the situation, take responsibility for your "stuff' so you can move on and out. Take with you only that which is yours. Don't assume responsibility for the other person's "stuff." You can only move on with optimism when you deal with your issues and take your power back from those who might use and abuse it.

Remember, people who are doubtful about the future are more likely to try to push the adversity away as though they can somehow escape its existence by wishful thinking, more likely to do things that provide temporary distractions but don't help solve the problem, and sometimes even give up trying. People who are confident (optimistic) about the future exert continuing effort, even when dealing with adversity.

Acknowledging Your Gifts

"Use what talents you possess. The woods would be very silent if no birds sang there except those that sang the best."

– Unknown

"If Raymond can't fix it," announced my father with conviction, "it can't be fixed." After an hour of trying to repair the pick-up on our Bamford BL50 square baler, Father and I were on our way to the local farm implement dealership. Raymond was the eldest son of the owner and an exceptional, natural mechanic.

When I posed the question, "How did Raymond get so good at fixing things?" my father paused for a moment, chewing thoughtfully on the toothpick in the corner of his mouth. "Well," he said after some consideration, "he's just got a knack for it." The look on my face prompted Father to explain further. "It comes natural to him. You know how some folks can just sit down and play a piano or pick up a brush and paint a picture? It's as if they were born knowing how to do it. It's that way with Raymond." I pondered my father's explanation. "Then it's a gift," I concluded. Father nodded as he geared down for the entrance to the dealership. "Yeah, that's what it'd be, a gift."

A gift or talent resides within each of us and along with that endowment, a longing for greatness. It's part of what makes us human – of what drives us to excel. Most people, though, have long since given up the quest for greatness. Money worries, relationships, work, school, and the pursuit of simple pleasures now consume all of their time and energy – while the pursuit of things higher takes a back seat.

It's not supposed to be like that! We were meant to use our gifts in our quest for greatness. Greatness is actually alive inside of you right now just waiting to be discovered. Living an empowered life is possible – even if you don't think you have the time, energy, youth, intelligence, or strength for it. Everyone has a gift – a talent – and, though it may never be realized, it is always there awaiting expression.

Acknowledging your gift is the first step, using it is the second. That said, here are two questions that most often follow: "I have a gift?" and "What is it?"

To discover your gifts, start by believing in yourself and trusting your intuition. Intuition is "knowing" something without necessarily understanding *how* you know it. Intuition is a form of inner guidance or "gut feeling" that allows you to know instinctively things that your rational mind simply can't comprehend. Pause for a moment to consider what it is that you enjoy doing and what hobbies or activities you find especially rewarding. Generally, it's something you find easy to perform and do especially well. Think of those times when someone has said to you, "You are so good at (activity)." These are all clues or messages your gift is sending out to you.

Once you've discovered and given expression to your gifts, there will be a natural temptation to compare yourself with others – especially in the beginning. Now, I'm not going to suggest that the world won't place you in a competition or before a set of judges. Certainly, if you're choosing to enter into a contest with others, your performance will be evaluated and compared to that of your opponents. What I am saying is your gift and talent – whether it places you on the stage or firmly in the hearts and minds of friends and family – is just as wonderful and valuable as your neighbors' are, so cherish it and use it!

By the way, it took Raymond (the mechanic) only a cursory glance at the baler to discover the problem. Within half an hour, we were back in business, making hay while the sun was shining. After all, isn't that what life is all about?

It's Inventory Time

"If we take the time, no matter how crazy and troubled we feel, we can find something to be thankful for."

– Terry Lynn Taylor, best-selling author of *Messengers of Light*

It was nearing Thanksgiving and the teacher of a rambunctious Grade 6 class was mulling over ways to teach the kids the concept of gratitude.

"We have much to be thankful for," she announced. "And this afternoon we're going to take inventory of our many blessings."

"I'm thankful it's nearly home time," came a voice from the back of the room. The classroom erupted in laughter and the teacher smiled, shaking her head.

"Here's more what I had in mind," she said, picking up a piece of chalk. "We can be thankful for our families, the food on our table, the home in which we live, the friends we have here at school." She wrote each on the blackboard. "Who can think of another?"

A hand in the front row shot up. The girl declared, "I'm thankful for my legs." More giggles. "My mom's best friend got in a car accident and now she's in a wheelchair," she said, turning around in her desk. "She says we take a lot of things for granted like walking – until we can't do it anymore."

The teacher nodded. "We each have so much to be grateful for and yes, often we take it all for granted." She studied the class. "What else might we be thankful for?"

Another child tentatively raised his hand.

"My dad says I should be thankful for a full head of hair 'cause someday I might not have any – like him." Everyone laughed, but everyone got the point. Soon every child was busily filling his or her list with items each could be truly grateful for.

How long would your list be if you took inventory of your blessings? What items might you include: family, friends, faith, health and the necessities of life? Those who have food, clothing, shelter and the freedom to worship as they wish have more than much of our world's population will ever possess.

Too often, we focus only on the perceived inadequacies of our life. I knew someone who once kept a homemade sign pinned to her bulletin board. It read, "Your life is great – you have so much to be thankful for. Take some time to acknowledge your many blessings and reflect on the bountiful nature of your life."

How long would your list be if you took inventory of your blessings and added one new item daily? Would you be amazed at the size of the list?

You have 1,140 minutes in every day. How would your life be different if you spent just 15 of those minutes daily giving thanks, just 15 minutes filling your mind with concrete examples of how fortunate you are? Most of us would discover even after a few days that the exercise was life-changing!

Let me share an exercise that I've used for years with amazing results. The first task I perform each morning upon rising is to reach into the drawer of my nightstand and remove my gratitude journal. I start each new page by writing the date then the following sentence stem: Today, I am thankful for.... Without exception, I am able to fill an entire page with reasons to be thankful and in doing so get my day is off to a positive start.

Christian mystic Meister Eckhart said, "If the only prayer you say in your whole life is 'thank you,' that would suffice." I suspect he is right.

Deserving Happiness

"Happiness is not achieved by the conscious pursuit of happiness; it is generally the by-product of other activities."

– Aldous Huxley, *Vedanta for the Western World*, 1945

Do you deserve happiness? Think carefully before you answer that question. Every day I meet people engaged in a desperate search for happiness convinced this elusive "state-of-being" lies between the pages of the next self-help book or comes packaged with a new job or relationship. I also meet those who have withdrawn themselves completely from the search, convinced that happiness is either unattainable or that they are somehow unworthy of experiencing it.

You've heard true happiness can only be found within, but that sounds more like a Zen riddle than a piece of practical advice. Over the years, I have come to believe that happiness is not something you deserve, but rather something you choose. Volumes have been written on this theme, so my list of insights isn't intended as final word on the subject. However, taking one, some, or all of these suggestions to heart and putting them into action may move you closer to choosing happiness for yourself.

Insight number one. Stop and take some time to understand what you're doing. Most of our lives are simply running out of control. It's as if we have our "pedal to the metal" and we don't know how to take our foot off the accelerator. Perhaps we're afraid of what will happen if we do. So, stop and look around you. Where have you been? Where are you at this moment and where do you really want to go?

Insight number two. Ask yourself, what is happiness? Do you know? One of the most important reasons to stop the frantic pace of your life is to answer this question. Once you've spent a bit of time on that one, move on to these: What will bring me happiness? How will I know when I've experienced a new level of happiness? What will it look like, feel like? What will be happening or not happening in my life when I attain it? Where do I want to experience more happiness: at work or at home, with family and friends? Write down the answers to these questions.

Insight number three. Handle life's details, those basic needs we all have: food, clothing, shelter and love. Is it possible to have true happiness while your outer life is in turmoil? Perhaps, but it's certainly going to be a lot more challenging. It's difficult to contemplate what will bring you true happiness when your stomach keeps growling.

Insight number four. Eliminate what detracts from your happiness. If you want happiness, eliminate from your life that which makes you unhappy. This may include toxic relationships, clutter around your home, unsatisfying work, excess weight, and so on.

Ultimately, the choice is yours! To be happy, choose happiness. To be peaceful, choose peace. To be free, choose freedom. This step is so simple in nature that its power can be easily missed. Make happiness a conscious choice – call it out and make it so!

Finally, remove the word "deserve" from your vocabulary. Moreover, teach no one that he or she deserves happiness or anything else for that matter. Do we insist a rose must deserve its own fragrance, the sun its own light, the ocean its water? Happiness is a natural state of being. When you are happy, don't ask, "What did I do to deserve this?" but rather say, "Thank you!" Gratitude is an affirmation – it attracts what it focuses on.

Pursuing Your Passion

"Only passions, great passions, can elevate the soul to great things."

– Denis Diderot, prominent French encyclopedist and leader of the Enlightenment

"How can I create a more positive attitude and sustain it?" That's a common question. My typical answer is this: you develop a positive outlook by disciplining your mind through repetition. You read positive material every day. You enjoy uplifting audio and video presentations. You associate with positive people. You use positive language.

However, there is another powerful technique to boost your attitude: pursue your passion. By passion, I mean an activity so engaging that when you do it or even speak about it, you get excited. You come alive. Your enthusiasm is boundless.

Allow me to clarify. You could be passionate about watching sports as a spectator, but that's not what I'm getting at here. I'm asking you to identify opportunities where you can actively participate. It doesn't have to be something where you work up a sweat. You could collect stamps, coins, or comic books. You could study local history and visit the museum and archives. You could write a book. Only you know what gets you energized.

I know what some of you are thinking. You're saying to yourself, "I know what my passion is, but it would be unrealistic for me to pursue it right now. I have a mortgage to pay. I have a family to support. It's just not possible for me to quit my job and do what I love." I'm not suggesting that you act irresponsibly. You don't have to quit your job to pursue your passion. Many people use this as an excuse, though. The truth is, you can treat your passion as a hobby at the outset. That's what I did. I loved reading about self-esteem and empowerment so much that I began to wonder how I could share this information with others. I was passionate about this information and wanted to do something with it.

Would I be correct in assuming most of you have a passion you're not following right now? Maybe you want to be a writer. Perhaps, you'd like to sing, form a band, or do stand-up comedy. Possibly, you have talent working with your hands, or you're a great cook who has created wonderful recipes. You just know that when you think about, speak about, or actually perform this activity, you feel passionately alive. Time seems to pass quickly. You're completely absorbed and in the moment. You're living in the now!

I believe we come into this life with special talents and express them in ways that nobody else can. In fact, you feel as if "something is missing" when you refuse to engage in that activity and keep ignoring the urgings to act. When you follow your passion, you'll be much more positive and excited about your life. That will transfer over into other activities as well. Moreover, you'll be amazed at what opportunities open up for you.

Consider this: nature does not give you the desire to do something and then not provide you with the ability or talent to do it. You might want to read that statement again. You have the desire to pursue this passion because it is something you were meant to develop and – more often than not – when you develop this talent and give expression to it, you make a positive contribution to the lives of others as well.

If You Want to Learn

"Learn to ask for what you want. The worst people can do is not give you what you ask for, which is precisely where you were before you asked."

– Peter McWilliams, best-selling author, poet, motivator

Let's imagine you wanted to become a professional musician. Your first step might be to hire someone to teach you and begin lessons. You could practice, then join an orchestra or band. You might read about musical things and accompany your musician friends to concerts. In short, you would support yourself in every way to realize this dream.

How much support are you giving yourself to realize the life you want right now?

As far back as I can remember, my mom has told me, "If you want to learn how to do something then talk to someone who is really good at the 'thing' you want to learn." She helped me learn that lesson when I was 17. My cousin Wayne asked me to be a groomsman in his wedding party. I was thrilled until the topic of a dance and grand entrance came up in discussion.

"Grand entrance?" I asked. "What's that all about?"

"Well," explained Wayne's fiancée, Sharon, "the bridal party arrives at the hall together. Wayne and I share the first dance and then the rest of you join us."

Panic struck me. I didn't know how to dance. I hadn't tried dancing since I was a kid, and then only with my mom after the community Christmas concert. I thought of bowing out of the wedding party, but I couldn't dream up a gracious way to do it.

Mom got on the phone and called her friend, Iris. Iris and her husband, Freddy, were the best dancers in our community. When they twirled around the hall, everyone cleared the dance floor, watched, and cheered. Mom knew Iris was the "someone" I needed.

A month before the wedding, I got off the school bus at the home of Iris and Freddy. Dance lessons would be for one hour every Monday and Thursday. Iris put a Don Williams LP on the console stereo and I watched as she moved with an imaginary partner to the music, counting each beat. *One*, two, three. *One*, two, three.

That first lesson was perilous – for Iris. We knocked knees and I stepped on her toes more than once, but throughout the ordeal, she remained patient and just asked me to start again. I felt like a fool by the end of the first lesson and giggles from Iris's girls didn't help. Word spread quickly and soon I became known on the bus as Twinkle Toes.

With Mom's encouragement, I persevered and soon I was moving awkwardly through the waltz steps and bouncing up and down to the polka, two-step, and jaunty schottische. On the day of the wedding, Mom brought our movie camera and filmed the grand entrance. When I watch that old Super 8 movie and I see myself gliding across the dance floor with my bridesmaid partner, I can still hear Iris's gentle words of encouragement.

The lesson here is an echo of my wise mom's words, "If you want to learn how to do something, then talk to someone who is really good at the 'thing' you want to learn." Ask for help to realize your dream – whatever it should be. If you happen to be an expert in your field, share your wisdom and mentor an eager student. You might end up with sore toes or bruised knees, but you may just help someone realize the life they desire.

Failure to Integrate

"What we know only intellectually may not actually influence our behavior. This [comes only] from a more integrated 'knowing' of mind, heart, and soul."

– Salanter, Lithuanian scholar

Have you ever met someone who could speak eloquently about lofty spiritual ideas, but whose own life and relationships were a mess? What about someone quick to give financial advice, but whose own financial fortunes teeter on the verge of bankruptcy? Without knowing it, these people reveal to us one of the greatest secrets in life: knowledge alone is not enough. In order for positive, personal change to occur, knowledge must be integrated into our lives and expressed in the form of action. Collecting knowledge is like collecting books: as your library grows so does the storehouse of available information. Failure to integrate new information into your life is like owning a vast library of books that you have never read – impressive, but only in outward show.

"Do as I say and not as I do," has become the unintentional mantra of many a well-meaning person. That said, we should never – straight-out – brush aside information from a person who "talks the talk" but fails to "walk the walk." The information may be beneficial – perhaps the exact insight or puzzle piece we've been missing. We are left, however, with the nagging question, "Why aren't these people taking their own advice?" We might think of somebody with a bad habit, for example, who "knows" that his or her habit is self-destructive, yet keeps on doing it. We say things like, "She should know better," and perhaps she does at an intellectual level – but that new information has never been integrated. To stop, she must emotionally internalize her desire to change.

In schools, teachers constantly face the challenge of having students integrate new information with what they already know. For example, when children first learn to read, they do so by recognizing letters and then the sounds they make. Once that information has been integrated, they can go on to recognize simple words. It's the same with enhancing our self-esteem: we must build upon what we already know and understand.

So, how might we begin to integrate new and useful information into our lives? Each person has his or her own preferred learning styles. In order to connect this new information to existing ideas, we need to answer questions. How does this new information relate to what I already know? How is it similar or different? How does it change what I know or think I know? In this process of integration, we need to apply new information and practice using it. It takes courage to consider new and radically different ideas – to contrast new and perhaps conflicting information with what we already hold to be true. Most importantly, integration requires you to be an active participant in the process, which means you must be motivated. Motivation occurs when you believe that what you are learning is interesting, important, and relevant to your life and current situation.

Some people can integrate new ideas and concepts quickly, while others take years to integrate fully a new concept. That's OK. People incorporate knowledge in different ways depending upon their background, life experiences, and level of understanding. It is not sufficient merely to "know" it; new information must be examined, considered, and tested in the real world. There is as much distance between "knowing" something and "setting it upon your heart" as there is between knowledge and ignorance.

Clarity of Purpose

"Clarity of mind means clarity of passion, too. This is why a great and clear mind loves ardently and sees distinctly what it loves."

– Blaise Pascal, physicist, mathematician, publicist

My friend Rhonda walks at a brisk pace. I discovered that one late summer afternoon while I scrambled to keep up with her on a walking path winding down along the Red Deer River. Rhonda is one of those unique individuals who knows exactly what she wants and where she's going – and she's not wasting a minute getting there. She has clarity of purpose that's evident in every aspect of her life.

Later, while massaging my sore feet, I began to ponder the advantages of having a clear and well-defined purpose. The old adage, "know thyself," has become such a cliché that it has lost much of its meaning. The fact remains, when we're completely clear on who we are, what we want and where we're going – and have a plan to get there – we become more effective, more successful, enjoy better health and a life that's fulfilling. Isn't that what we all really want?

Many people either don't know their life purpose or have misidentified it as what they do – assuming it to be their career/job/profession or primary role in life, such as being a good parent, spouse or employee. Don't get me wrong; those are crucial functions and should never be undervalued. However, consider this: doesn't it make sense that your life purpose would encompass all of your life, not just your work or the roles you play?

With clarity of purpose, life becomes a whole lot more fun. We find ourselves in the flow of life rather than resisting it. The most important thing we can do for ourselves is to invest the time, energy and perhaps even money to become clear on what we want out of life. This isn't always an easy process and perhaps that's why so few people do it.

Here's the good news: all of the information is inside us. We need only to think carefully and dig deeply in order to gain the insights we need. This simple process may help. Imagine you're seated across the table from yourself. Now ask the following questions:

- If you had the time, what would you most want to study, practice, master, or research deeply? In what area would you like to be known as an expert?
- What activities do you engage in or talk about and lose all track of time?
- For what particular skills or abilities have you received the most compliments?
- If money wasn't a concern, what work would you be doing?
- In what personal talents, skills, and abilities do you have the most confidence?

• What would you do if you weren't afraid?

Your next question might be, "Are you willing to pay the price for it (i.e., sacrifice, face your fears, break bad habits, make necessary changes, make tough decisions, handle the setbacks, etc.)?"

Rhonda shared with me that living life on purpose requires a lot of soul searching and groundwork. "I had to get my ducks in a row," she explained.

We want to know that our time here on earth has made a difference. More than just having our basic needs of food, clothing and shelter met, we also want to experience the higher values such as love, joy, happiness, a sense of fulfillment and accomplishment. Remember, your life purpose is the context, vessel, or container into which you pour your life. Your life purpose belongs to you and no one else. Only you can live it.

Setting Goals

"The reason most people never reach their goals is that they don't define them, or ever seriously consider them as believable or achievable. Winners can tell you where they are going, what they plan to do along the way, and who will be sharing the adventure with them."

– Denis Watley, author, speaker, motivator

Setting goals is a powerful technique used by successful athletes, businesspeople and achievers in every field. Goals give you long-term vision and short-term motivation. Understanding how to set and achieve long and short-term goals will help boost your self-confidence and build the framework for a lifetime of achievement and empowerment.

When you choose a goal, it is important to set one that's big enough to be challenging. My father used to say, "If a challenge doesn't scare you at least a little bit, it's not big enough." It took me years to understand what he meant by that statement. Set goals that are slightly out of your grasp now, but not so distant that there's no hope of achieving them. No one will put serious effort into achieving a goal that they believe is unrealistic or unattainable.

How do you begin? First, decide what you want to do with your life and what far-reaching goals you wish to achieve. Second, break these goals down into the smaller pieces that you must first achieve in order to reach larger goals. Lastly, once you have your plan, start working towards implementing it. Seek balance by setting goals in some or all of the following categories: attitude, career, education, family, finance, creativity, fitness, relaxation, and community service.

Express your goals positively and be precise putting in dates, times, and amounts so you can measure your successes. If you do this, you'll know exactly when you've accomplished the goal, and can take complete satisfaction from its achievement. Write goals down: this crystallizes them and gives them force. When you have several goals, give each a priority. This helps you to avoid feeling overwhelmed and directs your attention to the most important items on your list.

For far-reaching goals, establish where you'd like to be in 25 years, in 20, 15, 10 and so on. What would you like to accomplish in the next month, six months, and one year? Finally, draft a list of tasks you can do tomorrow to start moving you towards your goals. Bear in mind that your goals will change as you grow. Adjust them often to reflect this growth in your personality. If goals no longer hold your interest then let them go. Remember:

goal-setting is your servant, not your master. It should bring you pleasure, satisfaction, and a sense of accomplishment.

In order to move into something new, you have to let go of something old. The transition between these two states can be daunting. As you establish new goals and begin moving toward their attainment, old doubts and fears may claw their way to the surface – forcing you to look back, not forward. When you recognize that you've been at a certain fork in the road before, yet continue moving forward with confidence and without looking back, your next journey along this road will be smoother and more enjoyable. That part of your road will now be straight.

Enjoy the achievement of goals and reward yourself appropriately. Draw lessons where suitable and feed these back into future performance. Setting goals can provide clarity and purpose in your life. It can strengthen your resolve, enhance your self-esteem, and help you to let go of disappointing past experiences. It can guide you along a path of self-discovery.

Investing Your Energy

"The bedrock of all ambition is motivation, the definition of which is an intense and sustainable drive toward a specific goal."

– Linda Austin, M.D., author of *What's Holding You Back – 8 Critical Choices for Women's Success*

Investing your time and energy is like investing your money. If the risk is too great, you might lose it all! However, risk can spell the difference between getting what you want and sitting it out, between achieving your greatest desires and forever wishing and hoping. By making a responsible choice as to what activities deserve our time and energy, we can approach each task with both passion and purpose.

Time. It's our most precious commodity. With so many opportunities before us each day, how do we decide which task deserves an investment of time and energy? Start by asking yourself the following questions and provide an honest answer.

Can I learn from this experience? Can I grow as a human being by doing this particular activity? Will I acquire new skills, knowledge, or insight?

Who is depending on me to perform this task and why? Eventually any worthwhile endeavour will involve us with other people. Will this action bring me together with people in a worthwhile manner?

Will others benefit, and how? Will the activity be of benefit to my family, my neighborhood or community? The activity needn't be grandiose or imposing. An activity as simple as cleaning the house or mowing the lawn can return an investment: a more comfortable home and a brighter, more inviting neighborhood. An evening walk can return the dividend of a healthier body, clearer mind, and longer life.

Will I ever have another chance to do this again? Some opportunities are once-in-a-lifetime. Is this one of those rare occasions?

What will I have to put on hold to do this? What is the trade-off? How will it affect my immediate and future life? What sacrifices will I or those around me have to make so that I may perform this task? Other questions to ask may include, "Does this earn a living for me?" After all, in a material world, we all have financial responsibilities that cannot be ignored.

Do I feel obligated to perform this task? Are any of my activities the result of feelings of guilt or obligation? Society provides us with only a vague line between good manners and being taken advantage of by another. It's up to us to draw a clear line and stand strong.

Finally, can I have fun? Ultimately, if I don't need to do it, don't have to do it and can't derive at least some pleasure from it, then it's probably not worth doing.

Here's a point to consider. What are the odds that people who see an activity as boring, tedious, or beneath them will make a powerful difference in their community or the world? Moreover, what are the odds that people with a passionate, positive vision of what they hope to achieve will fail to make a difference?

By investing our time and energy wisely, we can reap tremendous rewards – physically, financially, emotionally, and spiritually. Moreover, we may discover – much to our delight – that we have much more time than we imagined. As my dear friend Dana, professional writer and mother of two active boys, pointed out to me, investing your energy is simply that – making wise choices every day. If you don't have the energy to do it, you probably need a break – and that's another idea for a column.

Assertiveness

"Assertiveness basically means the ability to express your thoughts and feelings in a way that clearly states your needs and keeps the lines of communication open with the other."

– John W. Travis M.D., Regina Sara Ryan, authors, *The Wellness Workbook – How to Achieve Enduring Health and Vitality*

Do you avoid speaking your mind then feel frustrated afterwards? Are you afraid if you do speak your mind, people won't like you? Perhaps you yell and demand to be heard – convinced your opinion is an undeniable truth. There is a better option and it's called being assertive.

Contrary to what you might believe, being assertive has nothing to do with being aggressive. Instead, it's about honestly communicating your thoughts, feelings and needs to others in a clear and appropriate manner. Communicating assertively can give your self-esteem a huge boost, help with relationships, making decisions, solving problems and resolving conflict. Assertiveness is the middle ground between passivity and aggression.

Most people are not assertive for fear of displeasing others and of not being liked. Although we may avoid some immediate unpleasantness by not being assertive, we can also jeopardize relationships and – most certainly – leave issues unresolved.

So, how can we become more assertive? What are the action steps? In my experience, four steps allow you to communicate assertively. Let's start with basic assertion. This is a simple, straightforward expression of your beliefs, feelings, or opinions. It's usually a simple "I want" or "I feel" statement.

Empathic assertion usually contains two parts: recognition of the other person's situation or feelings, followed by a statement in which you stand up for your rights. Here's an example, "I know you've been really busy, but I want to feel that our relationship is important to you. I want you to make time for me and for us."

Escalating assertion occurs when the other person fails to respond to your basic assertion and continues to violate your rights. You gradually escalate the assertion and become increasingly firm. It may even include the mention of some type of resulting action or consequence. For example, "If you don't complete the work on my car by 5 p.m. tomorrow afternoon, I'll be forced to call the Better Business Bureau."

I-Language Assertion is especially useful for expressing negative feelings. It involves a three-part statement. When you do . . . (a behavior), the effects are . . . (how the behavior affects you). I'd prefer. . . (what you want). Here's an example: "When you didn't buy the groceries when you said you would, I couldn't cook the dinner for my parents. I feel hurt and angry with you. Next time, I'd like you to follow through when you agree to do something."

Communication involves more than just the words we choose. It includes what we say, how we say it, and the body language we use. When practicing being assertive, maintain direct eye contact, keep your posture open and relaxed, be sure your facial expression agrees with the message, keep a level, well-modulated tone of voice, and select an appropriate time to be assertive.

Remember, there's more to assertiveness than getting your way or telling others "how it's going to be." You need to listen too, as others often have something important to add to the conversation. Assertive communication is like having a debate: both sides need to be listened to and respected.

Say what you mean and mean what you say. It's OK to tell people – in an appropriate and respectful manner – exactly what you think, feel, and want. Be clear about what you want to say, whether it is negative or positive. This will help stop confusion and misunderstandings. Being honest with yourself and others is a big part of assertiveness.

Avoiding Conflict

"Difficulties are meant to rouse, not discourage. The human spirit is to grow strong by conflict."

– William Ellery Channing, writer and Unitarian

In a recent management seminar, the facilitator spoke about a concept she called "Moving Away/Drawn Toward." She explained that some people are motivated by reward – they are the "Drawn Toward" group. These goal-focused individuals will set their sights on what they want – promotion, raise, or recognition – and relentlessly move toward the achievement of that goal. The "Moving Away" group is focused on what they don't want and typically, that's conflict or confrontation. The problem with a moving away strategy is that it's fear-based and always has you walking backwards – looking back. It's easy to trip and fall into the same situations you've been trying to avoid.

On the drive home, I had time to ponder my own tactics. It was sobering to realize my entire strategy for coping with work and life had been centered on moving away.

If that's you as well, then don't be too hard on yourself – you've probably spent a lot more time focusing on what you don't want and have a pretty clear picture of it in your mind. If you're ever going to live a truly empowered life, you will need to embrace a new approach, as focusing on what you don't want will simply bring more of it into your life.

Sure, there are times when avoidance is a good strategy. Avoiding might take the form of diplomatically skirting an issue until a better time or withdrawing from a threatening situation. I was aware enough to realize my moving away strategy was not serving my best interest. I vowed immediately to begin focusing on what I did want in my life.

After years of running backwards, how could I possibly turn around, turn my back on what I didn't want, and start moving in the direction of what I did want in my life?

I started by listing all the things in my life that had me feeling frustrated and fearful – the things I didn't want or was afraid to face. For you, these items could include a stressful job, your children's behavior, regret, guilt, or conflict in your relationships.

Next, I made a list of all the positives. For each situation on my list, I found everything I could think of that was positive in the situation. For example, a difficult job may also bring the benefits of income, creative challenge, or personal growth. The job can be a vehicle for expanding your level of patience. At the very least, it could bring you the valuable information that this isn't what you want to be doing with your life.

I chose to maintain a positive attitude. This didn't mean I pasted a smile on my face. It did mean that I worked at feeling grateful for what I already had and for what I believed would come. I shifted my focus from feelings of lack to feelings of gratitude and abundance. I began to believe in myself, in the future, and the positive changes in my life.

I began to visualize a better life. I made a detailed list of what I wanted in my life because, up to that point, I don't think I really knew what I wanted. Each day, I sat down and visualized what my new life would look like and how it would feel to have the changes.

I worked hard to ensure my thoughts, feelings, and behavior were all in alignment with my goals and not my fears. Over time, I began to think, feel, and act differently.

Turn your back on what you don't want – turn around and face what you do and find yourself drawn toward a new life of empowerment, gratitude, love and abundance.

Say "Yay!"

"Each person has an ideal, a hope, a dream which represents the soul. We must give to it the warmth of love, the light of understanding and the essence of encouragement."

– Colby Dorr Dam, author and motivator

Many years ago, when my daughter Bethany was about four years old, she asked me to teach her how to shoot hoops. She'd watched some older boys in the neighborhood tossing balls and thought the game looked fun.

We drove to the local hardware store for a hoop and basketball. Upon returning home, I nailed the basketball hoop above the big door on our garage and attached the net. As best I could, I demonstrated the finer techniques of shooting the ball through the hoop. After a few successful shots, I asked Bethany if she was ready to try it. She said she was and I handed her the ball.

"Dad," she said to me, "when I throw the ball, you say 'Yay,' OK?"

I smiled. "Do you want me to say 'Yay' if you get a basket?"

"No," she replied. "You just say 'Yay' whenever I throw the ball."

I agreed and we had a wonderful afternoon tossing the ball and plenty of fun cheering each other on. My daughter was not afraid to ask for the encouragement she needed. In time, she became quite adept at shooting hoops. Perhaps we all have something to learn from her.

Inspirational author and educator Brian Cavanaugh relates a story about the devastating effects of discouragement. Dante Gabriel Rossetti, the famous 19th century poet and artist, was once approached by an elderly man who asked him to look at his sketches and drawings. The gentleman wanted to know if the artist thought they were of any value. As gently as possible, Rossetti told the man that the sketches were of no value and showed little talent. He apologized for the harsh assessment but said that he believed he should be honest. Obviously disappointed, the old man nodded and sighed.

Before turning to leave, he asked the artist if he could look at just a few more, which were all done by a young art student. Rossetti looked over the second batch of sketches and immediately became enthusiastic over the talent they revealed.

"These," Rossetti said, "Oh, these are very good." He went on to say the young student showed great promise and should be given every help and encouragement. "This student may have a great future as an artist if he will study and work hard."

The old man was deeply moved.

"Who is this fine, young artist?" Rossetti asked. "Your son?"

"No," replied the visitor sadly. "It is I, 40 years ago. If only I had heard your praise then. For you see, I became discouraged and gave up too soon."

How many times, at a critical crossroads in your life, has someone offered you a word of encouragement, a hug or a listening ear? How often have you been the one to provide the affirmation that brightened someone's day? It's safe to say the world would be a better place if we all took time to pass along the power of encouragement.

Mother Teresa wisely said, "Kind words can be short and easy to speak, but their echoes are truly endless."

Your encouraging word, given today, may forever change a receptive life.

Sometimes, all you need to say is, "Yay!"

Empathy

"The great gift of human beings is that we have the power of empathy."

– Meryl Streep, actor and political activist

At one point in my 30-year broadcast career, I worked for Canada's largest entertainment company. I used to say that my job of managing "creative" people was a lot like herding squirrels. Even more reason for me – at the time – to be an effective leader and role model.

The other day a friend and I entered into a discussion on leadership. He manages a large and successful local business. He told me strong leaders understand the difference between empathy and sympathy. Sympathy is the act of sharing the feelings of another – a harmonious agreement or accord as in, "He is in sympathy with their beliefs." Empathy does not mean agreement. Empathy is when we understand and acknowledge another person's thoughts, feelings, or actions – especially in an emotionally charged situation. Quite simply, people who demonstrate empathy can put themselves in the other person's shoes. It doesn't mean they know exactly how the person feels – they may never have been through a similar experience. Nonetheless, they appreciate that the individual is experiencing strong feelings.

Let's say a single parent arrives at work having been up all night with a sick child. This employee comes to work because she has a great attitude and work ethic. The supervisor, who is single with no children, can demonstrate empathy by making a statement like, "You must be worried about your son. Let's get this report done so you can check on him."

People who don't understand nor appreciate the concept of empathy can be recognized by their rigid attitudes and statements, which often have a devastating impact on the self-esteem of the distressed individual. If you can't or won't speak to another's feelings, you run the risk of being viewed as distant, aloof, or insensitive. Many a transaction, interview, sale, or relationship has been torpedoed because one person didn't feel heard, valued, understood, or appreciated.

People who lack empathy will tend to gossip, criticize, or keep notes about people without taking the time to understand the other's world or get a sense of the issues that need to be addressed. Even worse are those people who try to appear empathetic but really don't care. Their insincerity and deception can be seen from a mile away.

How can you demonstrate empathy? Learn to identify your own feelings. The better you are at identifying your feelings, the more effective you'll be at identifying the feelings of others through language, facial expression, tone of voice, and body language. It takes practice to identify properly the feelings of others. Let people know you sense where they are coming from. As you're speaking with people, get in the habit of making notes and then feeding back your observations. Empathy could sound like this.

"It sounds like you're *snowed under* with what's happening here at work."

"You seem *pleased* with the decision that we've just made."

"You appear *disheartened* by the changes here in the office."

"I think you're *optimistic* about the new job opportunity."

When you acknowledge the feelings of others, you validate them. This validation translates into a feeling of being heard and understood. Demonstrating empathy is a powerful relationship-building skill that can help repair a damaged personal or business relationship and enhance a strong and healthy relationship. Be empathetic, be genuine and you'll be perceived as warm, supportive, and understanding.

Identifying = Understanding

"You must look into people, as well as at them."

– Lord Chesterfield, aristocrat and British diplomat

The man dropped into his recliner chair with a beer in hand. He reached for the remote only to discover that his wife was already holding onto it. She was watching television – a movie – one of those chick flicks. Worst of all, she was crying. Annoyed at his sentimental wife's constant sniffling, he spouted, "What's with you? Why are you crying about the imaginary misery of people you don't even know?"

His wife replied, "For the same reason you yell and scream when a man you've never met scores a goal."

That reason, of course, is that we identify with the person or the event. The word "identify" originally comes from the Latin root "idem," which means "same." When we identify with someone, we feel the *same* sorrow or joy and we understand the dilemma. There is no substitute for the ability to identify with others.

For years, my Aunt Lillian worked at a busy local hospital as the head dietitian. Her days were spent planning the meals for each patient in the hospital and it was a job she took seriously.

"I always considered myself an empathetic person," said my aunt, "someone who could reach out and understand what others were going through. Then I became a patient when I was diagnosed with ALS (Lou Gehrig's disease) and realized I never really knew the meaning of the word 'empathy.'"

Regretfully, many of us only come to this understanding during difficult or heartbreaking times. My aunt came to appreciate how a simple smile could mean so much to someone sick and terrified about what was happening in his or her life. She discovered the joy of having someone take a few minutes and be friendly, talk, and show genuine interest.

"I hate this disease," she once said, "but it has taught me so much!"

My aunt had worked compassionately and professionally for years, but in the end had a completely new dimension of understanding added to her life. She learned to identify with patients, family, and friends. She knew how they felt and responded to them differently. She hated what the disease was doing to her body, but seldom complained. Though the time of initial diagnosis until the end of her life was less than three years, she remained positive and strong in her faith, displaying tremendous courage and character.

You may never help patients in a hospital, but I'm sure there's someone in your life who could benefit from your ability to identify with that person's pains and pleasures, wild dreams and dashed hopes. Best-selling author Dean Koontz once said, "Some people think only intellect counts: knowing how to solve problems, knowing how to get by, knowing how to identify an advantage and seize it. But the functions of intellect are insufficient without courage, love, friendship, compassion and empathy."

It is a rare person who has cultivated the ability to clearly see inside others and identify with them. Nevertheless, it's crucial to living an effective and happy life. So feel free to stand up and cheer when your team scores the winning goal, or to sit back, sniffle and shed a tear when a book or movie moves you. It's all part of being an empathetic person. Thank you, Aunt Lillian for identifying with each of us and sharing your wisdom and understanding.

Gossip

"Whoever gossips to you will gossip about you."

– Spanish proverb

Gossip. What is it? That's the easy part. How to deal with it? That's the hard part.

Gossip is information about a person, true or false, that is spread around from one person to another – often becoming distorted, retooled, and embroidered upon in the process. Remember the whispering game you played in school: take a statement and whisper it to the person in the desk behind you? By the time the statement had traveled through the classroom, it was often significantly different. It's the same with gossip.

Some gossip is forgotten in a week. Other gossip is remembered for a lifetime. Nearly all gossip is destructive. It can destroy friendships and relationships, lower morale in the workplace, add stress to your life and affect your ability to make positive life choices. Gossip can hurt your feelings, negatively affect your self-esteem, and in extreme cases lead to depression, fear, anxiety, or self-destructive behavior.

In a society often fixated on rumors and sensationalism, gossiping may seem entirely acceptable. Tabloids, talk shows, and tell-all biographies are everywhere! People like to hear funny, disturbing, embarrassing things about other people. Gossipmongers revel in the misfortune of others – feeling the need to bring someone else down to their level. Choosing to see others in a negative light allows them to *appear* better by comparison. Threatened by the success of other people, gossipmongers cast aspersions rather than accept responsibility for self-evaluation and positive change.

Gossip can become a habit. You may gossip without realizing that you're doing it or understanding the potential for harm. If you're an active contributor to the gossip mill, you need to stop to consider why. Is it simply a habit or are there deeper issues at play? Do you find certain people or situations threatening? It is worthwhile to spend some time considering why you gossip and what benefits you derive from the activity?

There are two sides to consider when dealing with gossip: the giving side and the receiving side. There is no sure-fire strategy to end gossiping, but there are things you can do to lessen the impact. The first and obvious one is to ignore it. Easier said than done, right? Some gossip is hard to ignore. Even if you ignore it, it can still cause damage. You can try to clarify the situation with a more accurate version of what was really said or done as long as doing so doesn't make the situation worse. (Keep in mind: truth and logic have little to do with gossip.)

If you have "sensitive" information about another person, keep it to yourself. If you feel the need to vent, choose a friend you can trust who has no stake in the person or situation. Try to put yourself in the other person's shoes. Would you like that information to be shared?

Perhaps your best choice is not to take part in the gossip at all. In fact, let it be known that you don't appreciate gossip and choose not to participate in it. That simple statement may be just the wake-up call that gossipers needs to hear. If nothing else, they will certainly avoid gossiping in your presence and that's a good start.

Finally, remember this simple rule: "If you don't have anything nice to say then don't say anything at all."

Energy Leeches

"The constant stress that flows from a negative attitude saps one's energy, focus, and motivation. It is hardly a formula for success."

– Chuck Gallozzi, author, speaker, motivator

The other day, a friend told me he'd come to a realization. Certain people always showed up in his life when he was feeling disheartened or in a negative state of mind. Why did they show up? Was he sending out an invitation calling them home?

All people come into our lives for a reason – to provide us with a message, a lesson, or an insight. Negative thoughts and actions attract negative people and situations into our lives. Perhaps the arrival of these people is simply a cue that our attitude needs to change. Whatever the reason, avoid the temptation to allow such people – Energy Leeches – back into your life. If you let them in, they will suck the life out of you. Here are a few tactics employed by Energy Leeches.

Negative comments: "I hate my life and work! Did I tell you what "so and so" did/said to me? Did I tell you what terrible thing happened to me the other day?"

Dream snatching: "You can't do that. Who do you think you are? Are you living in fantasyland? Get back to the real world. You should do this instead."

Put-Downs: "What is wrong with you? Can't you do anything right?" In other situations, the words may be less harsh, but the result ends up being the same. Once an Energy Leech attaches itself to you, it can be difficult to remove it. Instead, neutralize an Energy Leech the moment one arrives.

These strategies can often prove effective when dealing with a Leech in your life. Sometimes, however, the Leech lives a lot closer to home. Look in the mirror – sometimes we are the Leech. If we pay attention to our thoughts and words, we can eliminate the Leech within us. Are you being negative or positive? Ask yourself this question daily.

Confront and Reform: Tell your Leech that he or she is being negative. He or she may not even realize it. Ask for support, positive feedback and encouragement instead of put-downs. If your Leech is a colleague, family member, or friend, perhaps you can reform him or her into an Energy Addict. Show him or her how to spread positive energy. If your Leech just doesn't see it or refuses to do it then you may have to give an ultimatum. You might say, "This is my goal. This is where I am going and if you're going to be negative then I can't be around you."

Turn on the Light: When you were a child and afraid of the dark you turned on the light and felt better. Negative energy is like darkness. When you encounter an Energy Leech, turn on the light. When a Leech comes at you with fear, negativity, hate, and anger turn on the light and act in response with love, kindness, and a positive outlook. Negative energy is powerless in the light. Think about what happens when someone gets mad and yells at you. If you don't yell back, but remain calm, the aggressor often loses momentum and power. If you return with kindness, he or she will lose even more power. On the other hand, if you yell back at the aggressor, then the negativity grows and expands – soon enveloping both of you.

You should seriously consider avoiding Energy Leeches, as they will be of no benefit to you. More than likely, they will, drag you down to their level. Choose instead to associate with positive, empowered, ambitious people, as their influence will be of great benefit to you. You will learn from them, get support and encouragement from them, and they will provide you with opportunities you may otherwise not discover on your own.

Wise Mind

"Truly successful decision-making relies on a balance between deliberate and instinctive thinking."

– Malcolm Gladwell, *Blink: The Power of Thinking Without Thinking*

Most of us are familiar with the serenity prayer, "God grant me the serenity to accept the things I cannot change, courage to change the things I can, and wisdom to know the difference." The serenity prayer beautifully captures the essence of Wise Mind. To appreciate Wise Mind, you need to understand two states of mind: logical and emotional.

Logical mind. Fact and reason are the framework of logical mind. This intellectual or scientific state of mind defines reality in terms of facts, numbers, equations, or cause and effect. Balancing your checkbook, baking a cake, and doing a crossword puzzle are examples of logical mind at work. People high in logical mind are often decisive, calculating, and not prone to snap judgments or decisions – these are the serious, dependable people of the world. Although logical mind is critical to dealing with reality effectively, many of life's problems have an emotional aspect.

Emotional mind. If logical mind runs "cool," then emotional mind runs "hot." When an emotional state controls your thinking and behavior, emotional mind has taken over. Acting the way you feel is how emotional mind behaves. Strong emotions can distort facts, magnify excuses, and shrink your perception of consequences. Of course, a certain amount of emotional mind can be beneficial. Intense love is a motivation for intimate relationships. Intense devotion or desire motivates staying with difficult tasks and sacrificing oneself for others. A mother running into a burning house to save her children is in emotional mind. People high in emotional mind are often passionate about people, causes, and beliefs – these are the dramatic, fun people of the world.

Wise Mind is the active integration of emotional and logical mind. Wise Mind brings together the cold reason of logic and the heightened power of emotion into a centered and calm state of mind. To illustrate further, imagine a seesaw. When the seesaw is perfectly balanced, you're in Wise Mind. Now, think of a stressful situation. If the seesaw is tilted and logic is high, emotion will be low. We may appear aloof, detached, or cold. If we tilt the seesaw the other way and emotion is high – logic will be low. We may appear reactionary, impulsive, and defensive.

We've all been in emotional situations and afterward found our heads filled with all the things we "should have said." Had we been balanced in Wise Mind, those words or ideas would have come easily to us. Depending upon the situation, we each have a tendency to move automatically toward either the logical or the emotional mind. That's fine – go where you go. However, recognize where you are and then come back into balance.

Wise Mind is *being in the present on purpose*. To start using Wise Mind, practice identifying problems in your life and then bring them together with your experience, knowledge, and intuition. The ability to link your problems with your rational, logical abilities is the basis of Wise Mind. Mastering Wise Mind will allow you to get suddenly to the heart of a matter. It is grasping the whole picture instead of only parts – seeing or knowing something directly and clearly. It is calmly "feeling" the right choice in a dilemma, when the feeling comes from deep within rather than from a current emotional state. Such is the beauty and power of Wise Mind.

Coping with Depression

"It's not things that upset us – it's our view of things."

– Epictetus, eminent Stoic philosopher

Depression is a symptom of something out of balance in your life. Always look at depression as a warning signal from your body telling you some aspect of your life is out of adjustment. Anyone can become depressed following an unfortunate combination of circumstances. Prolonged depression can impact your self-esteem – affecting the way you feel about yourself, your eating and sleeping habits, and the way you view the world.

Surprisingly, many people won't seek help for depression – perhaps believing they should be able to manage personal difficulties on their own, others because they feel embarrassed and ashamed or perhaps because they don't believe they deserve help.

You should be aware of the signs of depression – in yourself and others.

- Sadness or irritability.
- Difficulty concentrating.
- Lack of energy, enthusiasm, or motivation.
- Restlessness or agitation.
- Change in eating or sleeping patterns.
- Feelings of guilt or worthlessness.
- Withdrawal from friends, family and previously enjoyed activities.
- Personal put-downs and negative self-talk.
- Disregard for personal safety or well-being.

It can be difficult to talk about feeling depressed until you realize it's a common ailment. In the latter half of the 20th century, depression increased dramatically among people of all ages. Research has revealed that many people (about 40 percent over any six-month span) suffer periods of sadness or melancholy. It's normal to feel "blue" or "down" occasionally. If you've been feeling low for more than a few weeks or are having difficulty functioning in daily life, you may be suffering from depression.

There are a number of things families and friends can do in the case of simple depression. Acceptance and belonging are crucial, so encourage the depressed individual to:

- talk to someone trustworthy,
- ask for help (from a parent, counselor, or doctor),
- spend time with friends,
- participate in sports and hobbies,
- call a 24-hour crisis help line.

Prevention of simple depression is also possible. There is a range of skills and activities that everyone can do that will maintain a positive state of mental health.

- Do things that will improve self-esteem. (Join your local Self-Esteem Society.)
- Encourage positive thinking by associating with people who have an optimistic outlook on life and themselves.
- Manage your social skills. By getting out and getting involved, you are working on such skills as problem-solving, communication and confidence – skills that will help make and keep positive friendships.
- Develop good peer relationships.
- Set goals then go for them.
- Eat well, exercise, and get adequate sleep.

Depression and stress are often linked. Depression may surface when we have suffered losses, when we are coming to terms with changes in our lives, or when we are over-taxed physically. Stress is a part of life, but it can impair our physical and mental well-being.

Simple depression is a common ailment. It is not unusual and it's not permanent. Never accept any present mood as permanent. Clinical depression is a far more serious condition and may require professional treatment and counseling. The first step in fighting depression is to understand what it is, how it affects you, and what causes it. To learn more about depression and treatment, contact the mental health office nearest you.

Guilt

"Peace visits not the guilty mind."

– Juvenal, Roman satiric poet, author of the *Satires*.

The world is filled with people living in a needless state of constant guilt. I know that's an over-generalization, but how many people do you know whose daily lives are guided by guilt? A friend or family member who feels guilty if she spends a penny on herself? Others who feel they must be constantly responsive to the needs of others? How about the individuals who feel guilty if anything goes wrong in the life of a loved one – convinced they could have prevented it? And what of those individuals who feel guilty just for being alive? Does this sound like someone you know – yourself, perhaps?

First, understand that you are a good and worthwhile person, deserving of love and attention, and you're not being selfish when you choose to nurture yourself. Whether you're taking some time to rest and rejuvenate, read a good book, watch a movie, spend some money on you, or eat a slice of chocolate cake, you don't need to feel guilty!

So how can you lessen or even prevent those times of overwhelming guilt? Start by not allowing others to impose their values upon you. When you were young and didn't understand right from wrong, you needed someone to establish values for you. Perhaps the time has come to re-examine, re-evaluate and revise your current values to ensure they reflect your beliefs and not the views of someone else.

Most people who suffer from unnecessary guilt do so because there is a critic (metaphorically) sitting in their head. This critic may use the voice of an angry parent, a judgmental teacher, a mocking sibling, or someone else who judged the person as a child.

When your behavior is based on your own values and decisions and you hear the critic whispering guilt into your ear, smile and say, "Thanks for sharing," and tune it out. When you reflect back on past choices, understand that you did the best you could with the tools you had at your disposal. You could have done nothing more. If you now realize that it was not enough, reach out to get some better tools, tools to help you become more of who you really want to be, to help you do what is right.

The only way to make right the past is to make right the present. When making choices, ask yourself, "Do I wish to be known for this behavior?" Examine your motives. Why are you considering a particular action? If you will eventually need to explain your actions, will you be honest about it? If you don't want others to know about something you're considering, let that be a signal of impending guilt and don't do it! If you're still in doubt, talk with someone you trust who will give you an honest opinion.

Remember, your mistakes are nothing but the trials and errors of a life spent learning. Allow yourself the luxury of being wrong and forgive yourself for not being wiser and more aware. Forgive yourself for acting consistently with your limited awareness and forgive yourself for the damage you caused because of not knowing. Allow yourself to be human.

The Pressure Cooker

"When life comes to feed, make sure you are not the main course"

– Dannye Williamsen, author of *The Metaphysical Minute*

When my brother and I were small boys on the farm, mother brought home the latest truly amazing kitchen contrivance: a pressure cooker. It was an odd-looking contraption with its heavy pot and equally heavy lid. Most peculiar was the little knob that sat on top of the spigot that blossomed out of the center of the lid.

Mother announced that she'd be making baked beans, one of my father's favorites, and we could watch if we liked. Preparing the beans was a big job, but when they finally went into the pressure cooker – well, that's when the fun began. Once heat was applied, this astounding new kitchen convenience became a steaming, spitting monster of a pot, noisily rattling on the kitchen stove – the little knob dancing on a plume of steam.

Sensing danger or perhaps, and more likely, having lost interest, my brother and I retreated to the living room. That's when the phone rang and that's when it happened. A loud bang rudely interrupted mother's call, resulting in beans on the floor, beans on the ceiling, beans on the walls – you get the big messy picture.

For many of us, life is made up of a thousand little capitulations and humiliations, words not spoken, emotions not expressed and issues left unresolved. We don't realize how much hurt and disappointment we press down into the depths of our psyche so we won't have to acknowledge it. It's like being inside an emotional pressure cooker. The more of our emotions that we force into submission, the greater the force of the explosion when they come out – and they will!

When I was young, it took a great deal to push me into an angry outburst. When that threshold was reached however, the explosion was always exponentially more intense than the action that sparked it. As I grew older, I discovered why: the explosion represented the cumulative effect of many such actions that I had stuffed down inside me.

After one memorable and frightening outburst I asked myself, "How long have I been swallowing all of my anger, hurt, and fear?" Do you know what I figured out? It didn't really matter when it started. What did matter was that I recognized that I was doing it and started trying to change it by becoming the Witness.

Becoming the Witness requires consciously noting when you have a negative reaction to any situation, such as shouting at someone, or simply feeling frustration, regret, hurt or anger over the way something unfolds. The Witness steps back from the initial event – effectively creating a gap between event and response – takes note of what happens, how you feel about it, and how you react to it. The Witness does all this without making excuses, beating up on you, or taking score. It takes time and serious effort for this process of self-observation to become second nature to you, but it will.

Such a proactive stance on your personal psychology increases your awareness of the connection between your thoughts and feelings and your subsequent actions. It also gives you something specific to work on. Thus, it reduces the pressure that is building inside you from all those suppressed feelings!

These actions will lead to taking personal responsibility for your life experiences rather than blaming them on circumstances or other people. They move you from being someone who reacts to one who responds, able to choose consciously how you answer to life's challenges.

Understanding Anger

"If you would cure anger, do not feed it. Say to yourself: 'I used to be angry every day, then every other day, now only every third or fourth day.' When you reach thirty days offer a sacrifice of thanksgiving to the gods."

– Epictetus, eminent Stoic philosopher

Anger is a normal emotion experienced by everyone. Anger can make your hands shake, your voice tremble, your mouth go dry, and make it difficult to focus on what the other person is saying to you. Anger and the resulting guilt can have a devastating effect on the self-esteem of all parties engaged in the conflict.

People experience anger in different ways and for different reasons. While feeling angry is a natural reaction to situations that hurt or upset us, it is important that your anger be expressed in a productive way. Letting your anger build or explode can have a negative effect on your mental and physical health. It can be just as deadly to swallow the anger, bottle it up, and allow the negative energy to devour you. Anger turned inward expresses itself physically – ulcers, hypertension, and migraines can be results of internalized anger.

When you're angry, take time out, and cool down. When you feel angry, take a couple of deep breaths before responding to the person or situation that made you upset. Taking this time will clear your head, bring you back into balance, and help you avoid saying or doing things you will regret later.

Discover what's making you angry. We are seldom *just* angry; often something else is going on in our lives. People get angry when they are hurt, upset, disappointed, left out or frustrated but often only let their anger show with no insight into the reason for the flare-up. After you've cooled off ask yourself, "What is really going on here"?

Is one thing or are many things making you angry? Are you angry with yourself, with others or about a situation? Is the current situation an excuse to release pent up anger? Watch for your anger triggers. What sets off your anger? When you become angry, is it typically directed at one person? Are you directing your pent-up anger toward your children or other family members – people who may be unable to defend themselves against the onslaught? If you do "lose your head," you'll have to take responsibility for your words and actions. If you don't, you're likely to lose friends and the respect of others.

When you feel angry, write your thoughts on paper. Write down everything that you feel and why you feel it. This can be an effective way to relieve your anger and discover ways of tackling situations that upset you. Write a letter to the person you are angry with, but do not send it! This is especially good if you store your anger, allowing you to release it productively.

Don't ignore other people's anger. Listen to what they have to say and try to find out what is making them feel that way. Remember, it may have nothing to do with you. This does not justify their outburst, but it may alert you to what is really going on. Be careful about giving your own advice or opinions in case they are not welcome.

Remember, anger is not always a bad thing and can work positively for you and others. Throughout history, anger has motivated people to change things in their world they didn't like such as social injustice, discrimination, pollution, and cruelty.

Finally, if someone's anger is resulting in violent or abusive behavior toward you or loved ones, remove yourself as quickly as possible from the situation and seek professional support and counsel.

Bury the Hatchet, But Not in Your Neighbor's Back

"Don't carry a grudge. While you're carrying the grudge, the other guy's out dancing."

– Buddy Hackett, comedian

I once knew a man by the name of Otto. A hard and driven businessperson, Otto drove most people from his life with his critical nature and sharp tongue. One day, Otto told me of a business deal gone sideways. He spoke of how the person involved had lied to him and not delivered on his promise. As the story progressed, Otto grew more and more enraged. His volume increased, his face turned red, and he banged his fists on the tabletop. The intensity of his emotion startled me and I was prompted to ask, "Have you tried speaking to this person? Does he realize how upset he has made you?" To this Otto spat, "I can't talk to him – he's been dead for 20 years!"

At one time or another, you've probably found someone's behavior or intentions unforgivable. However, carrying a grudge is counterproductive. Grudges drain your energy – not the energy of the person for whom you carry the grudge. Bottled up anger can heighten physical stress, contributing to heart disease, ulcers, and other health problems.

You may believe that holding onto resentment will prevent you from being taken advantage of again. Ironically, a grudge sustains the illusion of having control while actually making you more vulnerable. Carrying a grudge can blind you to opportunities for happiness, enlightenment, and career advancement. In addition, grudges can provide excuses for not dealing with your own problems and shortcomings. It's often easier to find fault with someone else instead of seeing the role you played in the incident.

Check your internal dialogue for grudge talk. Here are some common examples.

Grudge talk: If I'm nice to others, they should be nice to me.

Counter argument: It would be great if the world worked that way, but it doesn't. I'm wise enough to realize that life isn't always going to be fair.

Grudge talk: This person is evil and deserves my hatred.

Counter argument: This person is human, like I am. He will have bad days and problems in his life I don't know about. I can't control all the difficult people I meet, but I can control how much I let them get to me.

Letting go of a grudge is actually healing. Finding a more constructive way to deal with your feelings is the key – you don't have to wait for the offending person to apologize. As with Otto's case, the person may be dead. As long as you nurse a grudge, you won't think about constructive solutions to the problem. Your grudge "blinds" you. Expressing your hurt and asking for an apology (if possible) gives you practice in assertiveness.

Banish your grudge from your life. Write out your feelings about what happened to you then destroy or burn the letter. Talk your feelings through while recording them on a cassette – fill both sides of the cassette if necessary. Yell, curse or cry – get it all out. When you've finished, drop the tape in a recycling bin for plastics. Imagine your grudge turning into something positive and constructive, like sturdy playground equipment.

Whatever personal ritual you come up with, the important thing is to concentrate on the wonderful feeling of letting go of the grudge. It is only through the process of letting go that you gain genuine control over your emotions and your life.

Dealing with Frustration

"I was angry with my friend: I told my wrath, my wrath did end.
I was angry with my foe; I told it not, my wrath did grow."

– William Blake, poet, from *A Poison Tree*

Frustration. We know how it feels. Here's how Webster defines it: the feeling that accompanies an experience of being thwarted in attaining your goals. Feelings of frustration are often intensified if other people cause the obstacles, if the goal is important, if you are close to achieving the goal, or if you have had many frustrations recently. Keep in mind, a goal can be something imposing or something as simple as crossing the street.

You may have heard the saying, "Frustration leads to aggression." Direct aggression is expressed toward the object perceived as the cause of the frustration. If a pop machine doesn't work, you might hit it or kick it. If someone gets in your way, you could verbally threaten or push the person aside. You might verbally assault him or her under your breath.

If the source of the frustration is too powerful or threatening for a direct approach, displaced anger may result. You may lash out at a less threatening and more available object. There can even be an entire "chain" of aggression. If the boss reprimands the husband, a direct confrontation may be too risky. Instead, he may criticize his wife for not having dinner ready on time. If the wife doesn't want to deal with her husband's aggression, she may displace her feelings toward her daughter, who has not cleaned up her room. Rather than challenging Mom's authority, the daughter may yell at a younger brother, who comes in to "borrow" a CD or game. Then the younger brother might kick the dog. (Perhaps the dog could bite the boss and complete the chain!)

Aggression is not the only response to frustration. Escape, withdrawal, and apathy are often employed. When repeatedly frustrated, people can drop out of school, quit jobs, or move away. The abuse of drugs or alcohol is a futile attempt at withdrawal. Apathy is giving up all of your goals, so you cannot be frustrated by your failure to reach them.

There are productive ways to deal with frustration. One of these is perseverance – steadfast persistence in adhering to a course of action. If at first you don't succeed, try, try again. Look at the life stories of successful people. Whatever the field – essentially all were frustrated in their early attempts to succeed. With consistent efforts, experience and luck, they finally made it. For instance, Thomas Edison had repeated failures before he found something that could function as a filament for the first incandescent light bulb.

When viewing the success of others, people often envy their fame and fortune. In contrast, they are rarely aware of the repeated frustrations and the hard work that led to their success – not to mention the continued effort that is still required.

Alternate methods to goal achievement can also be constructive. For example, on a walk, suppose you encounter a wall that blocks your path. Should you kick the wall and curse at it? No, you should reconsider your options. Is the wall low enough to jump over it? Can you climb over it? If these options are unavailable, you could search for a gate. If there is no gate, you might simply be able to walk around the wall.

Frustration, like stress, results from resisting the moment. Relax. Accept and assess the situation, consider your options, then – instead of allowing frustration to overwhelm you – search for an alternate means of achieving your goals.

Overcoming Fear

"Courage is resistance to fear, mastery of fear – not absence of fear."

– Mark Twain

Fear is an important emotion that alerts us to perceived danger – a survival instinct preparing us for fight or flight. Generally, we regain composure shortly after the fear is triggered, but, if fear begins to control us as in the case of anxieties, panic attacks, traumatic reactions, or phobias, our lives are no longer ours.

Not surprisingly, fear is the major barrier that most people have to overcome. Some fears are specific as in: fear of heights (acrophobia), fear of water (hydrophobia), and fear of dogs (cynophobia). Others exist as a vague uneasiness lingering in the background of every situation and conversation. Common culprits are fear of rejection, of making decisions, change, challenges, confrontation, loss, and failure. It is fear and all of its counterparts – worry, anxiety, and self-doubt – that paralyze us and prevent us from succeeding in life.

Conversely, some degree of fear can be beneficial. For example, when taking a test, performing, or tackling a new challenge, a measure of tension can stimulate a successful outcome. While phobias and other irrational fears may require therapeutic intervention to achieve resolution, generalized fear can be lessened with some simple techniques.

Avoid negative self-talk. Indulging in negative self-talk is one sure-fire way to derail your confidence – planting the seeds of uncertainty in your subconscious mind and causing your life and goals to become clouded with anxiety. Drop the words "can't," "won't," "don't" from your vocabulary; replace them with words like "can," "will," and "do."

Tune out negative comments by others. The next time someone tries to deter you from accepting a new challenge by use of negative remarks and questions, remember: the individual expressing the comment may be motivated by a fear of his or her own.

Imagine yourself succeeding in the stressful situation. Create a mental picture of the stressful or fearful situation and imagine yourself moving through it smoothly and successfully. This visualization will act as a dress rehearsal – allowing you to approach the situation from various points of view. For example, if you're fearful of speaking in public, imagine delivering your speech with confidence and then enjoying the adulation of the audience. It's a simple, yet amazingly powerful technique – try it!

Surround yourself with positive and empowered people. One of the best ways to overcome fear and boost your self-confidence is to connect with others who are doing the same thing. If you want to write a book, but have heard that it is difficult to get it published, consider joining your local writers club. You get the point. Surrounding yourself with others who have a positive attitude and similar interests will keep you on track, instill personal motivation, and help you to overcome fear by chasing away doubt.

Remember to practice deep breathing, which carries oxygen to the muscles and the brain, helping to calm fears, allowing you to perform better physically and think more clearly with greater focus. Keep in mind, it's not always necessary or desirable to eliminate fear. Learn to identify the gremlins that derail your confidence and shake your self-esteem. By recognizing your fear "triggers" you can learn to work alongside the emotion, instead of allowing fear to distract you and shatter your concentration. Once you learn to understand your fear, you will have gone a long way in achieving your dreams.

Hug the Monster

"Fear is a question: What are you afraid of, and why? Just as the seed of health is in illness, because illness contains information, your fears are a treasure house of self-knowledge if you explore them."

– Marilyn Ferguson, author of *The Aquarian Conspiracy*

In the summer of 1969 and again in 1972, my family traveled to Golden, B.C. to visit our aunt, uncle, and cousins. The visits meant a drive through the treacherous Roger's Pass. Mother hated the pass and clung tight to her purse for most of the slow, winding drive. Father used to tease mother about her nerves.

"Oh, Albert," she exclaimed, "I get terrified when you race around those curves."

"Then do what I do," he suggested. "Close your eyes!"

We are all afraid at times, but closing our eyes is not always the best way to deal with fear. Better to open your eyes and face those fears head-on.

In 1972, David Miln Smith had such an opportunity. Smith, an adventurer, author and professional speaker, decided to test his courage by spending a night alone in St. Michael's Cave on the Island of Gibraltar. In his book, *Hug the Monster*, he tells of hearing strange sounds all around him as he lay there in the pitch-black, damp and deserted cave.

Fear became panic, as Smith grew convinced that he was not alone. Then suddenly, as he was approaching his psychological breaking point, Smith thought to himself, "Whatever the monster looks like, I will hug it." That simple, almost silly thought brought great relief to his troubled mind. He soon fell into a deep and peaceful sleep until morning. Smith learned that embracing his fear, literally or figuratively, allowed him to subdue it.

Someone once told me that fear is simply "false evidence appearing real" and the only way that you can overcome it is to look straight at it. Start by sitting down and interviewing your fear. What is your fear, where does it come from, and why do you fear it? Once you understand your fear, you can start brainstorming methods that will help you best face it and work through it.

A friend once shared with me his debilitating fear of dogs. He reluctantly admitted, the mere sight of a dog caused him to have a panic attack. Inquiry revealed that when he was a child, his parents often visited neighbors who owned a small, ill-tempered dog. On one occasion, my friend walked into the neighbor's kitchen for a glass of water and startled the dog while it was eating. The dog bit him on the leg – leaving a physical and emotional scar.

He became convinced that all dogs were ill tempered and dangerous. A couple of additional incidents reinforced the belief. Only when he faced his fear and spent time with some friendlier canines, was he able to be around dogs again without panicking. Knowing where his fear came from was the biggest key to understanding it.

We each have our nights of fear. We each encounter monsters of one sort or another. We may fear spiders or snakes, heights or crowds, success or failure, the future or death. The next time you're afraid, try "hugging the monster." Confront that fear head-on, whatever it is, and embrace it. You may be surprised at how quickly it slips away and at how much more confident you begin to feel.

As Eleanor Roosevelt once said, "You gain strength, courage, and confidence by every experience in which you stop to look fear in the face."

A Laughing Matter

"I think we are never braver than when we stand tall and look into the sun and laugh."

– Linda Ellerbee, American TV journalist

Laughter is the best medicine and research now confirms the fact. It's difficult to remain stressed, tense, or uptight when you're holding your sides from laughter.

According to psychologist William James, we don't laugh because we are happy. Rather, we are happy because we laugh. The happiest people alive are those who know how to laugh often and well. What happens when you laugh? Your brain produces endorphins, which are neurotransmitters of happiness. Laughing is also contagious. When you get a group of friends together and one starts laughing soon all will be laughing.

Dr. Lee Berk and fellow researcher Dr. Stanley Tan of Loma Linda University in California have been studying the effects of laughter on the immune system. To date their published studies have shown that laughing lowers blood pressure, reduces stress hormones, increases muscle flexion, and boosts immune function by raising levels of infection-fighting T-cells, disease-fighting proteins called Gamma-interferon and B-cells, which produce disease-destroying antibodies. Laughter also triggers the release of neurochemicals, the body's natural painkillers, and produces a general sense of well-being.

Laughter establishes or restores a positive emotional climate and a sense of connection between two people, who literally take pleasure in the company of each other. A healthy sense of humor allows you to laugh at yourself and current life situation. Laughing at yourself can be a way of accepting and respecting yourself. Studies indicated that lacking a good sense of humor is directly related to lower self-esteem and higher stress levels.

So, how can you develop or boost your sense of humor? A sense of humor is developed by putting time, focus, and energy into experiences that make us laugh, feel good, and happy. The tips below can help you add to your capacity for laughter.

- Look for the everyday humor. Start looking for the absurd, silly, bizarre activities that go on around you every day.
- Observe infants and young children to learn how to find delight and amusement in the most ordinary of things.

• Increase your exposure to comedies, sitcoms, joke books, comedy clubs, etc.

• Hang around funny friends, or better yet, marry a funny partner.

• Take a five- to 10-minute humor break each day. Read jokes, add to a humor notebook, and listen to a funny tape or CD.

• If you hear a joke you really like, write it down, or tell it to someone else to help you remember it.

• Spend time with those who help you see the bright side and whenever possible avoid people who are negative and depressing.

• Avoid conversations, news, entertainment, etc., that frightens, upsets and distresses you or makes you feel sad and unhappy.

• Remind yourself to have fun.

Next time you feel stressed, look for the humor in the situation and laugh your heart out. Here's something to consider: By the time a child reaches nursery school, he or she will laugh about 300 times a day. Adults laugh an average of five to 15 times a day.

We're given the power of laughter, not only to laugh *at* things, but also to laugh things *off*. We'll always know difficulties, but happy people learn how to laugh most of them off and that's the reason they're happy – it really is a laughing matter!

Dealing with Loneliness

"They're sharing a drink they call loneliness, but it's better than drinking alone."

– Billy Joel, from *The Piano Man*

With a world population exceeding six billion, it seems peculiar that anyone should be lonely. The Internet, cell phones, pagers, and wireless devices are everywhere, but in the midst of all this technology, many of us still find ourselves alone. Our lives are teeming with people when all we really crave is intimacy – the certain knowledge that someone knows who we are and cares about what happens to us. The real epidemic of the new millennium isn't physical but spiritual in nature: it is loneliness and isolation.

Loneliness, at its core, is a feeling of detachment. New situations can trigger loneliness: the loss of a partner, a move to a new community, children moving out or leaving home for post-secondary education. Conversely, loneliness can creep in when relationships become repetitive or routine. Boredom and loneliness often go hand in hand.

So, how can we begin to "reattach" and resolve our feelings of loneliness? Start by reminding yourself that loneliness is not a life sentence. You have a choice in the matter, but a release from this self-imposed prison will take a commitment to action on your behalf. During the course of a day, look for ways to get involved with other people. Put yourself in new situations. Engage in activities in which you have genuine interest. You will be more likely to encounter the kind of people you are interested in meeting – people with whom you have something in common.

Develop your social skills. Get to know others and let them get to know you. Don't judge new people based on past relationships. Try to see each person you meet from a new perspective. Remember, intimate friendships usually develop gradually as people learn to share their inner feelings. Avoid rushing into intimate friendship by sharing too quickly or expecting that others will. Value all of your friendships and their unique characteristics rather than believing only a romantic relationship will ease your loneliness.

For some people, loneliness stems from not knowing the "appropriate" things to do or say in a social setting. If this is a concern for you – check out the local bookstore or library for guides on etiquette, interpersonal relationships, and effective communication.

Strive for personal development on a physical, intellectual, and spiritual level. Be certain you follow habits of good nutrition, regular exercise, and adequate sleep. Use your time alone to discover yourself. Think of it as an opportunity to develop independence and to learn to take care of your own emotional needs. Use your time alone to enjoy yourself rather than just existing until you will be with others. Consider joining a local self-esteem society. Deal with your situation actively. Avoid deciding ahead of time how you're going to feel about any activity. Keep an open mind.

Doing things that help you to feel more "connected" can make all the difference when it comes to coping with loneliness. Keep in mind, loneliness can be a healthy signal. It can stir us to make changes – to begin a process that may increase social contacts, improve relationships, and explore activities that offer learning and growth. These activities needn't always involve others, as we can feel content or connected even when we are alone.

Sociability

"Sociability speaks to who we are, to what it means to be a human being, and says that we are social beings whose existence is not complete unless we care for others, and are in turn cared for by them."

– Kristen Monroe, author, editor, University of California

My father was one of the most sociable people I have ever known. He could sit down and strike up a conversation with anyone. What amazed me was his unique way of remaining totally focused and completely engaged in the exchange. People loved to visit with him. My father was a great listener and an interesting man – he could just as easily captivate an audience as emcee at a wedding reception as have a group of friends over for a pot of coffee – which he often did. He loved to laugh and it seemed to me that his laughter was always genuine and contagious. My father embodied the term "sociability."

In his influential book *Cooperation: The Basis of Sociability*, the late Michael Argyle states that our ability to cooperate and socialize provides emotional rewards such as joy, happiness, job satisfaction, affection and social support. This was certainly the case with my father, who seemed to derive tremendous enjoyment and a tangible boost in his energy level from a good visit. Argyle goes on to say the benefits of cooperation and being socially adept include better task performance along with a greater desire for personal development – ultimately, a healthier level of self-esteem.

So, how does one become sociable or increase one's level of sociability? Is it a talent to be born with or a skill to be learned over time? Social skills are closely related to, and in fact somewhat dependent upon, good communication skills. A series of revealing questions may help you to assess your level of sociability and provide you with insights into your social awareness and the quality of your communications. Can you say with all honesty that you listen patiently to others and try to see things from their point of view? Do you openly discuss your feelings and share your opinions? Do you allow others to speak without interrupting or changing the subject? Can you tell the difference between a friend and an acquaintance?

An impromptu poll taken among some of the most outgoing people I know produced the following suggestions to enhance your sociability: leave the house; open your mouth; join a group or club; take up golf; learn to paint. Get out there and do it!

I can say from personal experience that your ability to socialize improves as your level of self-esteem increases and vice versa. As a child, I was reserved and often uncomfortable in social settings – in many ways, the opposite of my gregarious father. Recognizing my awkwardness, my father gave me a piece of advice I have come to recognize as the most profound, yet simple approach to understanding sociability.

He sat me down and he said, "Son, everyone has something of value to tell you." My first thought was, "Could it be that simple?" In the years that followed, I came to realize that the "something of value" could be an actual piece of information, sound advice, or an insight into life itself. A question I often ask myself is, "What have I learned about myself from this exchange?" With an open mind and heart, you'll be amazed at the insights.

By keeping this simple philosophy in mind, it became much easier for me to remain totally focused, engaged in the conversation, and be a good listener. And the more I practiced it, the easier it became. I discovered – as will you – that everyone really does have something of value to tell you.

Shine Your Light!

"Let your light shine. Shine within you so that it can shine on someone else."

– Oprah Winfrey, American talk show host

Growing up on a dairy farm in Northern Alberta provided me with plenty of opportunities to learn life's lessons. I recall a warm autumn evening when one of our best "milkers" went into labor. In a short time, it became apparent that something was terribly wrong. The calf was coming the "wrong way" and the cow was in distress. Mother and Father discussed calling the vet; an expensive cesarean section seemed the only option. Father pondered the idea before walking into the milk house and picking up the phone.

"Myrtle is coming over," he announced when he returned. Myrtle was a neighbor with a gifted understanding of animals – and kids, too as she had six of her own. A true earth mother, Myrtle was a hardworking, no-nonsense woman, barely five feet tall and a fireball of energy and opinion.

Within 20 minutes, an old pickup skidded to a halt outside our barn and from the dust stepped Myrtle, a galvanized pail in hand. She handed the pail to Father. "Fill it with warm, soapy water, please." She tossed an old towel over her shoulder and stepped into the barn.

Inside, she approached the cow slowly, speaking in gentle, hushed tones. She knelt down gradually by the animal – listening, patting, and probing. At last, she stood up.

"Breech," she said and father nodded. "I'll have to turn the calf – if I can."

That's when Myrtle pointed at the door. "Kids out!" she said. Father motioned with his head. We trudged outside and sat impatiently on a stack of hay bales – feeling, in an odd way like expectant parents.

About half an hour later Father pulled open the big sliding doors, put a finger to his lips, and motioned us inside. Myrtle was kneeling down, washing her hands and arms, the towel draped over her shoulder. While Myrtle washed up, the mother cow washed her perfectly healthy baby calf. Standing there, in the gentle glow of the barn lights, I felt certain a miracle had just happened. Later, when Father offered to pay for her time, Myrtle declined. "Just glad to help a neighbor."

Some years later, I heard the expression, "shine your light" and I came to realize that people give off their own kind of light. Not visible to the naked eye, but visible just the same. We speak of a "twinkle" in the eye or a "flicker" of warmth in the heart. Essentially, to shine your light means to share your knowledge, wisdom, and faith openly and honestly with the world and in doing so, making the world a better place. Some people shine with a light of kindness. Others emit a light of hope. There are those who glow with enthusiasm and still others who radiate love. Myrtle shone her light by freely helping neighbors in their time of need – whether with animals or kids.

All creatures are drawn to light. Do you want to attract people to you? Positive and life-affirming inner qualities attract people like a warm fire on a cold night. The light that will draw other people to you cannot be purchased in a store. People respond to that which radiates from within. You may not always see it, but your light is shining through. And it's one of your most attractive qualities! Shine your light!

Recognizing Opportunities

"Opportunities multiply as they are seized."

– Sun Tzu, author of *The Art of War*

The Royal Library of Alexandria in Egypt was once the largest in the world. Scientists and learned men of the time would visit the library from all over to study and add to the great collection. Most scholars agree the library was destroyed by fire (perhaps caused by an earthquake) but, to this day, the details of the destruction remain a source of controversy.

Many fables have risen out of the ashes. One such fable says that when the great library burned, one scroll survived. This scroll contained the secret of the Touchstone – a small stone that could turn common metal into gold. The Touchstone would be found near the seashore lying among thousands of other stones all looking the same. The secret to finding it? The Touchstone would feel warm to the touch; the others would feel cold.

The possessor of the scroll set up camp on the seashore and began testing stones. He knew that if he picked up an ordinary stone and simply tossed it aside, he ran the risk of picking up the same stone countless times again. Therefore, he devised a plan: whenever he found a stone that was cold to the touch, he would throw it far out the sea. Days stretched into weeks and the weeks into months. One day, however, about mid-afternoon, he picked up a stone and it was warm to the touch. Before realizing what he had done, he threw it far out to sea. He had formed such a strong habit of throwing each stone into the sea that when the one he wanted came along, he threw it away, too.

So it is with opportunity. Unless we are vigilant, it's easy to "toss away" an opportunity when it is right in the palm of our hand – and just as easy to miss it completely. One of the greatest challenges in our lives is seeing the forest and not just the trees.

The first step to recognizing opportunities is to be open-minded. Remember, anything is possible. When you are open-minded, you open yourself to a world of possibilities. Opportunities come in various forms. You may get a call from a friend telling you about a business opportunity. You may find an opportunity in the newspaper, on the radio or Internet – perhaps you'll overhear a conversation or get an intuitive twinge.

When you are presented with an opportunity, hold your skepticism at bay and explore the opportunity (again) with an open mind. Ask yourself, "How can I benefit from it?" "How many people have already seized this opportunity?" "Is this something I'm interested in doing?" Be sensitive to your circumstances – they are clues to your success. Your reality is your feedback mechanism.

The first test is to trust your intuition. Do you feel excited about a particular opportunity? Do you feel positive? Allow your intuition – your inner guidance – to lead you. The second test is your vision. Can you immediately see a mental picture of how this opportunity is going to unfold? The clearer the picture, the better the opportunity is for you.

When we open our mind, we break the cycle of habitual thinking. We recognize possibilities that, in the past, only came through hindsight. We stop tossing opportunities away and instead seize them, leaving others asking, "Why didn't I think of that?"

Intuition

"Our deepest fear is not that we are inadequate. Our deepest fear is that we are powerful beyond measure."

– Nelson Mandela, inaugural speech, 1994

Gut feeling. Sixth sense. Hunch. Subconscious thinking developed from your own experiences and rooted in your own beliefs. No matter what you call it or how you describe it, intuition plays an important part in the decisions we make every day.

Intuition comes from the Latin *intuitus*, "a look, to look at, contemplate." Many successful people started out with just an idea or thought – a gut feeling that a course of action was the right one. Most good ideas are based on good reasoning and intuition.

How many times have you had a decision to make and suddenly had a feeling of instinctively knowing what you must do? Intuitive messages appear in a range of ways such as a deep inner knowing, visualizing a clear and distinct picture, or a quiet, subtle nudge. It's important that you become familiar with how your inner self communicates and understand how these messages can bring a sense of confidence and empowerment. To grow, your intuition must be nurtured, exercised, and demonstrated, so be open to this power. Get past the ego that thinks you have everything figured out and be open to new possibilities. Here are some tips to help you get in touch with your own intuition.

- Watch for it. As you begin to recognize it, you'll have hunches and ideas more often. I recently bought a new car and now I see the same make and model all over town. The same will happen if you watch for your intuition – you'll start to see more of it.

• Question it. Try to see in which areas your intuition works best, or not at all. If your hunches about people or opportunities are generally correct, follow them.

• Feed your mind good information. Remember the programmer's maxim: garbage in, garbage out. Your skill, knowledge, and experience determine the potential effectiveness of your intuition. Learn about a subject before you expect any good hunches.

• Take a few minutes each day to experience inner silence. Calm your mind and clear your thoughts so that the information from your higher self can come through. Intuition is not something you can force – simply allow it to float up to conscious awareness. Give it time to work on challenges you face, be open to the possibilities and you'll be rewarded with increased awareness and perhaps an "Aha!" moment or two.

Your intuition will support your personal growth and help you through life's transitions. Begin by putting your intuition to work in small ways and eventually this "sixth sense" will become as natural to you as using any of your other five senses.

Here is my challenge: over the next week, make a list of all the times you felt the gentle nudge or sharp elbow of your intuition. Write down the times you listened to your inner guidance and those times you ignored it. Later, you can evaluate the results.

Intuition is a powerful force that must be embraced to work. Trust your hunches. Have faith in your inner guidance for both small decisions as well as major ones. Use your intuition in business decisions as well as the ones that affect your personal life. Develop your intuition so you'll never ignore it. How much better to say, "I had a feeling about that situation – thank goodness I trusted my intuition."

Act as If

"Act as if it were impossible to fail."

– Dorothea Brande, author

In the mid 1950s, a flamboyant but little known American pianist had dreams of performing in the Hollywood Bowl. He saved his money, rented the "Bowl" on an off night, showed up wearing a tuxedo and played a full concert on a grand piano to absolutely no one. Except for the empty hall, he had lived his dream. Then he kept striving until, four years later to the very night, Liberace performed at the Hollywood Bowl before a capacity, standing-room-only crowd. Liberace understood the "Act as if…" principle.

William James, the father of modern psychology, often taught the "Act as if …" principle to his students. He said, "Act as if *what you do* makes a difference and it will." He also said, "If you want a quality [trait], act as if you already have it."

When you hold a self-image firmly in your mind's eye, you will be drawn toward it. Choose the image carefully. Picture yourself vividly as defeated and that alone *will make victory impossible*. Picture yourself vividly as winning and that alone *will contribute immeasurably to your success*.

The "Act as if …" principle works especially well in the area of self-transformation. Whether you want to overcome shyness, kick a habit, find a fulfilling relationship, or achieve a long-held dream, the process is the same. Picture it in your mind then act as if you are already self-confident, free from the habit, or perfectly capable of finding that ideal relationship.

By acting as if you've already arrived, you train yourself and others to see you in a new light. Bear in mind, if your goal is, for example, to be a great manager, do some research first: talk to people and find out what great managers do, how great managers speak and conduct themselves. Then act as if you are that great manager. Don't make assumptions – do your homework.

Recently, a friend (we'll call him Jerry) expressed to his employer the desire to move into a soon-to-be available management position. Jerry felt he was ready for the challenge. He knew that two other staff members had expressed an interest – both more qualified than he and with previous management experience. Jerry asked if there was anything he could do to increase his odds. After some consideration, Jerry's employer suggested he act as if he already had the position.

"Act as if?" Jerry enquired.

"Demonstrate to us – by living example – that you are capable of assuming the position. Show us that you can lead, mentor, and direct." Jerry accepted the challenge and within a short time, a subtle change could be noted in Jerry's attitude, appearance, and deportment. He dusted off his copy of the corporate handbook and read it cover-to-cover, signed up for a college course on business leadership and time management, began to accept new challenges within his department, and assist co-workers with brainstorming and problem-solving. Over time, staff began turning to Jerry for advice and guidance. Eventually Jerry was awarded the management position. His colleagues were pleased with the appointment as they already saw Jerry as a natural leader.

Put the "Act as if…" principle to the test. Don't be surprised when the results are remarkable! Great living starts with a picture, held in your imagination of what you would like to do or be. What result are you trying to achieve?

Burn Your Boat – The Power of Commitment

"The quality of a person's life is in direct proportion to their commitment to excellence, regardless of their chosen field of endeavor."

– Vincent T. Lombardi, former Green Bay Packers coach

My friend Kevin is one of the most committed individuals I have ever met. Kevin is a one-man-show – an entrepreneur with a dream – and each year Kevin's business grows exponentially. To watch Kevin in action is to agree, his success appears limitless. He would be the first to tell you that commitment accounts for a big part of his success.

No great feat has ever been accomplished without a plan and a commitment to see it through to completion. Without commitment, we are defeated before we begin. There is no replacement for commitment. Failure to commit fully to a project or dream is a major cause of failure and a failing common to many people. Be honest: are you allowing fear, worry, and nervousness to govern your thinking? Do you find yourself habitually questioning your decisions? A lack of commitment creates self-doubt, leaves us emotionally drained, and ineffective. However, a lack of commitment can be overcome with effort. If you lack commitment, it's time to build a bigger fire under your desires and objectives.

Kevin was so committed to his entrepreneurial idea, that be burned his boat. Allow me to explain with a brief history lesson. It has been said that in battle, the ancient Greeks established a well-deserved reputation for bravery, discipline, and determination. Their success was built upon solid training, sound leadership and, most of all, commitment. The Greek commanders were master motivators who understood how to instill commitment and drive their soldiers to victory. The moment the Greek army landed on the enemy's shore, the commanders would give the order to burn the boats. Now, imagine the enormous psychological impact on the soldiers as they watched their only means of getting home set ablaze. There was no turning back. Once their boats were burned, the soldiers knew that the only way home was through the utter annihilation of their enemies.

In order to make his dream come true Kevin quit his full-time job. He risked it all and put himself in a position where success was his only option. He burned his boat. Like the ancient Greeks, Kevin understood the power and the absolute necessity of commitment. Now, you may not need to risk everything as Kevin did to fire your commitment. Kevin is honest about his radical "boat-burning" decision. It's simply this: he knew if he gave himself an out, he would take it. Do what you need to do to get committed!

In the pursuit of your dreams, your battles won't be fought on a distant enemy shore, but within the bounds of your own mind. Committed people are positive people. A truly committed person simply does not have the luxury or the time for the self-indulgence of negative thinking. Until you make the decision to be fully committed, there will always be hesitancy and the possibility to withdraw. The moment you truly commit yourself, things begin to happen. The true underlying motivation for all success is a deep and unwavering commitment to the dream. There is magic in commitment!

The possibilities for success are truly limitless for individuals who are fully committed to their dreams. If you are being bombarded mentally by thoughts of fear, anxiety, and worry, it may be time to "burn your boat" and become fully committed to your vision!

You Can Do It

"I believe that if I wanted to run a mile in four minutes I could do it. I would have to give up everything else in my life, but I could run a mile in four minutes. I believe that if a man wanted to walk on water and was prepared to give up everything else in life, he could do that, too."

– Stirling Moss, legendary British racing driver

In his best-selling self-help book, *The Five Secrets*, writer and motivator Pat Lynch tells the story of a visit to a kindergarten class.

"Who can skydive?" he asked the children.

Nearly all the hands in the classroom shot up. "Me – me – me!" cried the youngsters.

"Who can fly a jet plane?"

Again, a full showing of hands and more cries of me!

"Who can captain the space shuttle?"

The same response was provided by most of the children.

Pat makes the following point. He didn't ask the children, "Who would like to? . . ." He asked the children, "Who can? . . ." Children have a wonderful "can do" attitude. Although they may never have skydived, flown a jet plane, or captained a space shuttle, they believe they could if given the chance. A child's world is filled with endless possibilities. When Pat asked the same question to a room of adults not a single hand was raised. The point is our adult world is often filled with endless limitations – reasons why certain things can't be accomplished or shouldn't be attempted.

Sad fact: many of us approach life with a "can't do" attitude. Attitude, it has been said, is more important than aptitude. No matter how technically skilled you may be in your chosen field, you won't get far with a "can't do" attitude. Think you can or you think you can't, you'll be right. (You might need to ponder that last statement.)

A successful "can do" attitude involves three essential components: the ability to be a dreamer, a realist, and a critic. You need a good balance of all three to keep your attitude grounded. People often spend a lot of time dreaming or being critical. You need all three. Give yourself permission to dream. Stretch your mind to imagine the perfect outcome of that which you desire. Visualize yourself living your dream. Remember, there's a lot of truth in the saying, "You must see it to believe it." For something to happen, you must first allow for the possibility – in both your mind and imagination.

Now, take your dream and apply it to reality. Get into the habit of asking yourself how to make your dream come true and what steps you'll need to take to make it happen. Of your many dreams, decide which one takes priority then take action to make it happen.

Be your own best critic, not your own worst enemy. Great ideas and plans need to be challenged and inspected for strengths and weaknesses. Do this objectively. Don't make it personal. This isn't about you. It's about your plan. Look at each goal from every angle. If you like, get others to look for your blind spots. Iron out the glitches before you move forward. Road test it. Apply this approach to all new endeavors.

Finally, just do it! Get on with getting on! Start small if you like, but start! Then, keep going. This is what distinguishes can-doers from everyone else. Their "can do" attitude keeps them going. They may change strategy but remain true to their dreams. The most enduring overnight successes take years of preparation, planning, and hard work.

Perhaps you'll never skydive, fly a jet plane, or captain the space shuttle, but the next time someone asks who can do it, put up your hand and yell me, me, me!

Factor Number Four Summary: Effecting Change

Change begins with a choice. Many of us settle for far less than we're capable of achieving and can't understand why we feel so dissatisfied and frustrated with life. The truth is we have an inborn drive toward the realization of our full capability. Change in the hearts and minds of individuals can bring great and far-reaching results. Carry an inner will and courage to make a difference and become an agent of change.

Here are some questions and statements pertaining to effecting change that you may wish to ponder by yourself or discuss as a group.

1. Do I believe that people can change? Will I choose to be a living example of that change?
2. Do I commit myself fully to ongoing personal change – understanding that I will do my best each day and not criticize or judge myself harshly?
3. I acknowledge my many gifts and I use these divine endowments to make the world a better place.
4. I realize that each person is moving through this life as best he or she can with the beliefs and values each carries – I bestow no judgment and will assist when and where possible.
5. My life has purpose and as I release my false fears and self-defeating beliefs, I move closer to discovering my authentic self and living a purposeful existence.
6. I now look back over my life and see that each event served a purpose and brought with it a powerful lesson – guiding me to becoming a self-aware individual.
7. I no longer assume, but have the courage to seek clarity, ask questions, and discover the truth.
8. I choose to make as meaningful as possible the life that has been bestowed upon me, to live in such a way that I may be proud of myself, to act in such a way that some part of me lives on.

The Four Factors – In Summary:

So there you have it: four factors – four conditions that contribute either negatively or positively to our level of awareness and self-esteem.

Factor Number One: Early Programming

Beliefs are something we accept as true, without question. We live our life around them, often without thinking about them, questioning them or even being aware of them. An estimated 80 percent of our belief system is in place by the time we're 10 years old and only 10 percent of us will ever raise our awareness and re-examine those beliefs. Lack of awareness of a choice is the same as having no choice at all.

Factor Number Two: Reinforcement Of Belief

Despite our best efforts, we find ourselves repeatedly in the same kind of unhealthy relationship or stressful financial situations – unable to break free of a patently destructive pattern of behavior. Our seeming inability to resolve these patterns – based on false beliefs and values – can be demoralizing and affect our self-worth.

Factor Number Three: Self-Responsibility

To perform at your best and feel terrific about yourself, you have to be in a perpetual state of building self-esteem and maintaining it – pushing yourself beyond your usual mental and emotional limits. You need to take complete responsibility for the content and quality of your mind and the attainment of your dreams.

Factor Number Four: Effecting Change

Change begins with a choice. Many of us settle for far less than we're capable of achieving and can't understand why we feel so dissatisfied and frustrated with life. The truth is we have an inborn drive toward the realization of our full capability. Change in the hearts and minds of individuals can bring great and far-reaching results. Carry an inner will and courage to make a difference and become an agent of change.

Conclusion

Chris Cavanaugh – retired American freestyle swimmer and Olympic gold medalist once said, "Storytellers, by the very act of telling, communicate a radical learning that changes lives and the world. Telling stories is a universally accessible means through which people make meaning."

Allow me conclude this book with the tale of a wise and wonderful storyteller who came into my life at an early age. My Uncle Pat shared with me a fascinating life experience and with it, a strategy for living that has proven invaluable. The strategy: stick to it! The journey of self-esteem and empowerment (as with any journey worth taking) can be tremendously challenging. Stick to it – persevere. The learning is in the journey, not the destination. I have had many fine tutors in my life (my parents in particular). I know that many other amazing, empowered souls will join me yet on this great journey. Let me tell you a story now and, in the telling, perhaps change a life.

The River of No Return

Uncle Pat was an amazing storyteller. Puffing on his pipe, he would lean back in his chair and spin yarns that kept me captivated for hours. One of my favorites was about his brush with the stars – and death – during the making of the 1954 movie *The River of No Return* starring Marilyn Monroe and Robert Mitchum.

As a young man, Uncle Pat often drove truck to make ends meet. Incredibly, the trucking company Pat worked for was hired to haul cameras, props, and equipment for the new Otto Preminger film to be shot in the Canadian Rockies.

Pat described Mitchum as a "regular guy" who enjoyed sitting with the crew and truck drivers, swapping stories of Hollywood misadventure, and tipping back the occasional beer. Pat seemed taken aback by how small and fragile Monroe appeared.

"She seemed so sad," commented Pat, reflecting back. "And the way that director barked orders at her was awful. Sometimes, she'd just start crying and couldn't stop."

Pat had little time to be star-struck, however. The tight shooting schedule kept him busy loading and reloading the truck and maneuvering it down treacherous mountain roads. The bulk of the film was to be shot back at the studio, but Preminger wanted the outdoor shots to be realistic, and the rugged, unspoiled Canadian Rockies provided the perfect backdrop.

On one particularly cold afternoon, as Pat was guiding his overloaded truck down a mountain trail, the brakes failed. Within moments, he had a "runaway" on his hands. The truck was soon careening down the mountainside, the load shifting precariously with each curve Pat frantically manipulated.

"Jump," shouted the swamper. "You're going to roll it!"

"Shut up," yelled Pat and gripped the wheel tighter. Twice, it was nearly ripped from his hands when the big front wheels bounded over boulders along the trail's edge. At last, the road spilled out onto the riverbank and the truck rolled to a gradual stop on the gravel. Miraculously, no equipment was lost or damaged and shooting continued on schedule.

Pat would often tell me the secret to doing well in life was to "stick with it!" Never had he exemplified it as dramatically as on that occasion.

"Some folks just won't ride out the storm," he'd say. "They're too ready to jump."

People have always known that persistence and perseverance are key ingredients in success. Hence the old saying, "If at first you don't succeed, try, try again."

Recent psychological research supports the saying. Studies of successful entrepreneurs show that most (if not all) of these individuals possess a tremendous level of perseverance: they stick with it when the going gets tough and even when others yell to jump.

English biologist Thomas Henry Huxley once wrote, "Patience and tenacity of purpose are worth more than twice their weight in cleverness."

Single-mindedness, determination, dedication, self-belief and the inability or unwillingness to give in are what distinguish people who do great things with their lives from those whose dreams die with them. When you have great perseverance, you take into account what others say but you don't let it rule you. You remain true to your vision.

If I were to render my uncle's "stick with it" advice down to a simple equation, it would probably read, "Hard work + stick-to-itiveness = Success."

"Ride out the storm," I can still hear him say. "And don't be too ready to jump."

♦♦♦

About the Author

Murray Fuhrer is a full-time professional writer, speaker, and workshop facilitator – focusing exclusively on the topic of self-esteem and empowerment. His *Extreme Esteem Workshop* is a synthesis of the most powerful and life-changing tools and techniques he has collected over his career. Murray has had over one thousand articles, stories, and related materials published in local, regional, and national publications. A certified master hypnotist, Murray manages a thriving intuitive hypnotherapy practice and performs hypnotic stage shows – with a fun and empowering bent – at venues across Alberta. *The Four Factors* is the first in an anticipated series of books dedicated to the theme of empowered living. Murray has an unshakeable belief that the powerful message of self-esteem and empowerment needs to be seen, heard, read, and experienced by everyone.

Murray grew up in a small farming community in Northern Alberta. He and his wife Elke have five children and one delightful grandchild, Alexis.

"Stand back non-believers, 'cause I'm going to make it rain!"
Murray M. Fuhrer
www.extremeesteem.ca
www.theselfesteemguy.com